Off The Perch

United's rise and Liverpool's fall in the Ferguson Era

Mark Nevin

Contents

About the author

Mark Nevin began supporting United in 1974, when we were in the second division and Tommy Docherty was in charge. He later worked as a reporter on non-league football and published his first book on United in 2012, A Deeper Shade of Red, an autobiographical work detailing his experiences of growing up as a United fan surrounded, it seemed, by Liverpool supporters. This book in a way follows on from that one, but largely ditches the autobiographical stuff in favour of concentrating on the direct rivalry between United and Liverpool in the Alex Ferguson years. He still gets to most United home games and has contributed to several United blogs and websites. This year he launched a new United blog, United Roar: **http://unitedroar.blogspot.co.uk**.

Twitter: @DeepredMark, **https://twitter.com/DeepredMark**

Facebook: **www.facebook.com/mark.nevin.988**

For Tim

Acknowledgements

As usual, I'm indebted to all of those United fans who keep the Red Flag flying so proactively, especially those who kept the faith in Fergie in those days of 1986-1990 when, if we're honest, very few of us could see any light at the end of what was a very dark tunnel indeed. It has to be said: a massive thanks to the United board for keeping the faith. And of course, many thanks to the great man himself. I hope you'll forgive me for not using the 'Sir' prefix before his name throughout this book: I don't believe in the honours system and, as a proud socialist, I suspect he doesn't either. Finally, thanks to Liverpool FC for giving us all such a good laugh for most of the years covered in this book

Note on transfer information

Getting accurate information on transfer fees is fraught with difficulties. Information in this book has been drawn from from two sites:

http://manchesterunitedtransfers.blogspot.co.uk
www.lfchistory.net/Transfers.

Both of these sites are clearly well-researched and as close to being complete as I've been able to find across the web. Even here, though, there are bound to be problems in cases where transfer values have been kept secret and there are clearly times where the sources used are not completely reliable. Ultimately, I believe they give sufficiently sound data on which to base general conclusions about the transfer strategies of the two clubs, although some specific data may well be questionable.

Introduction

United v Liverpool in the Years before Fergie

Alex Ferguson claims he doesn't remember using the phrase 'knock Liverpool off their fucking perch'[1], although many of the writers who've attributed it to him claim he followed the remark with 'and you can print that.' Whatever its origins, the comment seems highly fitting for a man who, of all United managers, appeared to understand the nature and importance of the rivalry between the two clubs. Needless to say, he also possessed the fiery determination and obsessively competitive nature to do what no United manager since the seventies had managed to do – knock them off that fucking perch.

In addition to that spirit, Alex Ferguson also had the pedigree to produce football teams that were both combative and easy on the eye that fitted United like a glove. When he arrived in the autumn of 1986, United had just three FA Cups and a second division championship to show for their efforts in the period following the retirement of Matt Busby. It's often been said that United made a mistake in keeping Sir Matt at the club after his retirement, due to the shadow he inevitably cast over his successors. I've always held that view to be wrong. What United needed was a manager big enough to establish his own vision of the club whether Busby remained upstairs or not. if he couldn't do that, he wasn't big enough for the task anyway.

Tommy Docherty had appeared to possess that kind of character. Whether he'd have gone on to win the league at United had off-field circumstances not led to his removal, we'll never know. It was certainly the case, however, that the Doc managed to re-establish the cavalier model on which all truly great United sides have been based. At its peak, Docherty's teams consisted of two ball-playing central defenders: Martin Buchan and Brian Greenhoff, at a time when it was accepted logic within the English game that you had to have two guys back there who resembled club doormen more than footballers. His central midfielders – Sammy McIlroy and Lou Macari – were both former strikers who still possessed an attacking instinct. Yet, despite their flair and creativity, it could be argued that the Doc's United sides simply weren't combative enough to challenge for the game's biggest prizes. And, as his sides delighted footballing purists and United fans alike, a dour and methodical Liverpool side was emerging in the mid-seventies with the kind of winning mentality that mid-seventies United side lacked.

His replacement Dave Sexton found little affection among United fans. A cultured and quietly spoken individual, the lack of a brash and gregarious exterior was certainly a contrast to that of Docherty, which always gave him a lot of ground to make up in terms of establishing a relationship with the club's supporters. Although his defensive mindset has perhaps been over-stated in the years since, his introduction of Gordon McQueen at the back and Joe Jordan up front represented something like a capitulation to conventional footballing logic and it was this dismantling of the Docherty model, not to mention a lack of trophies throughout his time at the club, that were as much responsible his downfall as the cautious approach of his teams. Meanwhile, Liverpool continued to amass trophies, securing their third European Cup shortly after Sexton had been shown the door.

Ron Atkinson brought a return to a more cavalier model, and made United a consistent top four club again but, when he left n 1986, there was a feeling that he'd taken the Reds as far as he could and that the club was now in freefall. A ten-game winning run at the start of the previous season had promised much, but United had then crumbled spectacularly, eventually limping home in fourth place and, with United in the bottom four of the league in the following November, the board called time on his reign. Liverpool were again league champions under Kenny Dalglish and playing with a style that added considerable extra panache to the tried and tested models of Bob Paisley and Joe Fagan.

In many ways, what the board required from Alex Ferguson was a continuation of the style of Atkinson's teams but with added discipline both on the pitch and in the dressing room. Ferguson's reputation as a hard man suggested he was never going to tolerate the kind of off-field drinking culture that had prevailed under Atkinson. There was also a sense of the realist about him that, you sensed, was always going to add a stiffer spine to United's attacking spirit. His frugal character also suggested he wouldn't be tempted by the kind of quick fixes in the transfer market that had been one of the most problems of his immediate successor. This meant, of course, was that the Ferguson model would take some years to embed, something which it appears the United board always understood but which fans would take some convincing about.

But then Fergie clearly had other attributes that would see him through his difficult early years: an unshakeable conviction in his methods, an ability to inspire loyalty among the right kind of footballers and an extremely thick skin.

United fans of a certain age won't need reminding that Liverpool's experiences during that pre-Fergie period were rather different. In addition to their enormous trophy count, there was a sense of continuity that had eluded United ever since Busby's retirement. Yet a decline was about to set in, and indeed was far closer at the time of Fergie's arrival than anyone dared hope. And arguably its roots went back to the very beginnings of the dynasty established by Bob Paisley.

The Doc had only just brought United back into the first division when Liverpool boss Bill Shankly announced his unexpected retirement. Although his successor Paisley would go on to enjoy far greater successes than had the affable Scotsman, his more understated approach would mean he never rivalled the affection Liverpool supporters had for Shankly. Wisely, he didn't even attempt to because, as a motivator, Shankly was pretty much in a league of his own. Fergie himself was a massive admirer, often playing broadcasts of the former Liverpool manager to his Aberdeen teams for inspiration.

This practice might seem unpalatable to United fans of the modern day, but the truth is the affection for Bill Shankly always went well beyond Liverpool FC. Like Fergie, he was an avowed socialist and a man who valued loyalty to one's team mates above everything else in the pursuit of success. His tenure at Liverpool also pre-dated the intense rivalry between the two clubs, which really only dated from Liverpool's first European Cup win under Paisley in 1977.

Not only that, but Shankly loved United. In retirement, he heaped praise on the 'refreshing' and 'brilliant' football played by Docherty's teams [2]. Even in the years in which the immense rivalry between the two clubs took shape, he was a regular visitor at United's Cliff training ground and Old Trafford [3]. Yet he'd not been welcome at his former club since his retirement. Apparently fearing the same kind of problems that United had encountered after keeping Busby at the club, Liverpool had not invited Shankly onto the board and, despite his legendary status among Liverpool supporters, a distance had emerged between the great man and his club that only grew wider in the years after his departure.

This issue alone suggests that the alleged sense of continuity that Liverpool had enjoyed since Shankly's reign is a bit over-stated. They club certainly made a shrewd move in terms of appointing from within and the promotion of Bob Paisley is probably the greatest piece of of transition management ever carried out a top club. Yet that it only offered continuity at face value, which is probably one of the reasons why it was so successful,. Paisley was appointed from within the club, but he and Shankly were like chalk and cheese. This wasn't continuity; it was change management.

Bob Paisley's reign brought an inward-looking character to the club that, while successful, was scarcely lovable to the wider footballing public. Shankly's affable and media-friendly profile was replaced by a man who rarely even spoke to the press and favoured the concentration of debate within a small circle inside the club, combined with silence and secrecy in its dealings with the outside world.

Liverpool fans, as we would be reminded so often during Ferguson's mighty reign, were masters of denial. Rather than admit that their side's successful era that Paisley ushered in was based on dour conservatism, they sought instead to protect and nurture the Shankly image as the source of the true power of their dynasty. If Liverpool FC had a reputation for being successful but dull, this, they decided, was simply the projection of a hostile media envious of their club's greatness. Paisley's Liverpool largely ignored that media, deepening the trench mentality and making the accusations that the press failed to award their club the same amount of coverage as United on their back pages a self-fulfilling prophecy.

Yet, disregard it as they may, football was changing and signs that Liverpool were struggling to adapt to these changes were already there long before Fergie arrived in 1986. I still believe that the removal of Dave Sexton from United had far more to do with his reluctance (like that of Paisley) to engage with the media and the outside world. Liverpool had developed an insular and inward-looking approach that was anathema to United's fans. Sexton had been removed after a run of six consecutive wins and the allegation that declining crowds at United were the reason for his sacking are just not supported by the facts: although the five home games that season had been watched by crowds below 40,000, there had actually been some recovery in the last two homes prior to his removal. I've always believed it was the lack of an engaging public image that was the problem for Sexton. Football's media profile was about to be seriously cranked up in the coming years and an age in which it had to be accepted and, crucially, managed loomed far more heavily than at any time in the past.

For me, the Sexton dismissal showed that United had some awareness of this. Meanwhile Liverpool continued to plough on in their tried and tested way. It was an approach that was bringing them success, so why change? Yet skilled management always requires you to be more ahead of the game than that. It's what management types call 'jumping the curve': Liverpool decided the curve they were on was a perfectly good one and there was no way they were going to leave it for another one. The conservatism established within the club under Paisley made that inevitable. So, when Bob Paisley retired, they brought in Joe Fagan, a more personable character but still very much a member of the old school. Conservatism within the club became not merely a strategy to bring continuity but a conviction to be observed without question. Yet Fagan's age meant he could never be a long-term successor and revealed that the club were running out of home-grown solutions to the succession issue. Although there were younger members of the coaching staff available – such as Roy Evans, of whom more later – these were overlooked in favour of appointing Dalglish as Fagan's successor as in 1985, initially with Paisley as his assistant.

Paisley's return in this capacity indicated two things: one, that the club had a greater concern for continuity than they had when Paisley replaced Shankley and, secondly, that they acknowledged that Dalglish would need help from an experienced source. In the event, Dalglish always seemed caught between two eras. In terms of style, his Liverpool teams played with far greater panache than had the dour, conservative teams of Paisley. Secondly, he made a genuine attempt to drag Liverpool FC, kicking and screaming if necessary, into the modern world. His acquisition of John Barnes, the club's first black player, was a case in point. It succeeded brilliantly, the sheer quality of Barnes helping to silence crowds that had greeted him with everything from hostile scepticism to a hail of bananas.

Dalgish was, in his own way, attempting to address problems within the club that had lain unattended to since Shankly's retirement. In doing so, the ire of those racist fans wasn't the only hostility he faced. Paisley stepped down as Dalgish's advisor in 1987 and continued as a director and an increasingly critical one, as he broke the silence he'd maintained so effectively with the press during his own management career to express reservations about the direction in which Dalgish was taking the club in two notoriously caustic articles in 1989, for which he later apologized. [4]

Suddenly there appeared a tension behind the scenes at Anfield that had not existed, or at least not been made public, through the club's glory years. Unlike Fergie, who had the outward-looking Busby template still very much alive at the club against which to set his aims, Dalglish only had the insular Paisley model and it put him between a rock and a hard place. If he railed too much against it, he risked being accused of casting aside the club's successful formula. If he didn't embrace change, Liverpool risked stagnation in the modern footballing era.

In the event, he chose a middle way that succeeded in some areas but failed to stem an eventual decline the roots of which had been lurking under the surface for some time. His teams played with a style that made the old Liverpool approach seem very much a thing of the past. Off the field, however, changes were taking place that risked throwing out a highly successful baby with the bathwater. The dismantling of the club's renowned scouting network, for instance, meant the club were increasingly relying on his judgement, and that of a shrinking team of advisors, to unearth future talent. Initially this brought the fantastically successful signings of Beardsley and Barnes, so few were raising concerns at the time, but later ventures into the transker market were nothing like as successful. As the Dalgish era petered to a close and telling cracks began to emerge on the pitch, the signings of players like David Speedie and Jimmy Carter revealed a clearer and far less pberomising view of the future. Dalglish's resignation came as a surprise only because it occurred before the rot truly had a change to set in; a series of successors followed him into the murky recesses of the backwaters of the transfer market and, inevitably, come out smelling of shit.

At the other end of the East Lancs Road, Alex Ferguson was persuading United to crank up its scouting network and invest significantly in youth development. These were both hallmarks of the Busby era and thus managed to be both forward-thinking and fully in line with the club's traditions. United had reconnected with the past and, eventually, this would be rewarded with a glorious future. Meanwhile, Liverpool were entering an identity crisis from which they still haven't recovered.

Understandably, Liverpool FC will offer proof they were right to discontinue Shankly's involvement with the club in the form of a massive trophy haul. However, I wonder whether his continued involvement – and, following his passing, the involvement of someone with a similar outlook – might have made Liverpool still stronger, more outward-looking and ultimately better prepared to deal with the longer term challenges of a world that was beginning to pass them by even as they counted the medals and trophies.   Conversely, although Busby's continuation at United had attracted much criticsm, it enabled a different kind of continuity at the club.   Admittedly it was one that successive managers found it difficult to live up to but, when we found one who could, there was a sense of everything falling into place.

In Alex Ferguson, United found someone who could combine managerial expertise with a character big enough to move out of the shadow of the big man upstairs.   Rather than a successor to Atkinson, Fergie looked, and continued to look, more the successor to Busby. Graeme Souness, when he eventually took the reins of an already declining Liverpool squad from Dalgish, looked the successor only to a set of problems that completely lacked any set of solid traditions into which a new manager could blend.   It was this that truly pushed Liverpool off their perch.   Fergie's United then staged a glorious occupation that would last longer than any of us dared dream.

Notes
1. Alex Ferguson,Leading, p307
2. S. Egan, The Doc's Devils - Manchester United 1972-1977, p340
3. Alex Ferguson, My Autobiography, p37
4.Glasgow Herald, 2 March 1989, available at:
https://news.google.com/newspapers?nid=2507&dat=19890302&id=LD NAAAAAIBAJ&sjid=MlkMAAAAIBAJ&pg=3592,595812&hl=en

1

Choking Back the Vomit

Ferguson v Dalglish, Round One

26 December 1986

Liverpool 0 Manchester United 1

When Alex Ferguson travelled to his first game at Anfield, on the coach with him was former Liverpool manager Bob Paisley. That didn't signify a suddenly harmonious relationship between the two clubs: rather, it was a gesture aimed at preventing Liverpool fans from stoning the coach.

Despite Liverpool's dominance of the English game back then, United hadn't lost at Anfield since 1979 and previous manager Ron Atkinson had enjoyed a completely unbeaten record at the stadium. This did little to endear him to the Anfield faithful, who'd greeted him and his team on what would prove to be his final visit to the ground earlier that year with CS gas. Paisley's occupation of a seat on the team coach was simply an attempt to ensure it didn't happen again: surely even Liverpool fans wouldn't attack a United coach with one of their own on board? A wild presumption, perhaps, but it seemed to work.

Although a historical rivalry between their cities dates back at least to the nineteenth century, the intense United-Liverpool footballing rivalry we know today was barely a decade old when Fergie took the reins at Old Trafford. It often baffles younger Reds to learn that, when Liverpool played their first European Cup Final in 1977, the majority of United fans wished them well. After they'd won it, however, the rivalry really kicked in. Suddenly our status as the only English club to win the trophy had disappeared and when Liverpool played Bruges the following year, it was a completely different story, illustrated by United fan Tony Wilson sporting an 'FC Bruges' rosette when presenting Granada Reports on the evening of the final. In a matter of a year, the relationship between the two clubs had been completely re-defined, presumably for ever.

On the other side of the rivalry, Liverpool fans showed a baffling refusal simply to enjoy their dominance of the English game while it lasted. Instead, they chose to indulge a hatred of United that appeared to grow and become more intense with the more trophies they won. Its ugliest manifestation came in repulsive chants about the Munich tragedy that the club did little to stem or even to recognise the existence of at the time. The response to the CS gas incident was a belated attempt to come to terms with a vile element within its support that had somehow, via a sea of excuses, managed to survive even the Heysel Stadium massacre. Indeed, photographs at the stadium that day not only show the number of Munich flags and banners on display, but Liverpool players merrily chatting with the fans who held them. Liverpool fans will respond that United supporters sang distasteful things about Shankly's death and that's true, but it's difficult to imagine them, or any other club's fans, getting away with the displaying of distasteful banners like these on such a high profile occasion, let alone the apparent acceptance of them from members of the playing staff.

It would be difficult to imagine, then, that our new manager wasn't prepared for what passed for a greeting at the ground of the champions. Equally, while it's hard to say whether Alex Ferguson's obsession with, as he put it, 'knocking Liverpool off their fucking perch' had fully cemented at that time, he certainly could be in no doubt of the scale of the task that faced him. Liverpool had been English champions in eight of the previous eleven years. After several near misses, they'd completed a League and Cup double in the previous season and frankly looked as strong as ever, having added extra flair and guile to a traditionally well-oiled machine. In contrast, the United manager's first game had been a defeat at the mighty Oxford United.

This game came less than two months after Fergie's arrival at United and to claim that the jury was still out at that stage regarding his potential is something of an understatement. Although Ron Atkinson had failed to win United the league, his attacking brand of football had won him many admirers at Old Trafford and the question of whether Fergie's success north of the border could really translate to the rather bigger challenges below it had certainly been a major talking point at Old Trafford when his first game there, at home to QPR, brought a narrow 1-0 victory.

Wins in head-to-head encounters with Liverpool, however, offered much-needed relief for United fans in those days and thankfully Fergie's first team to play at Anfield were able to continue one of the few positive trends of the period. 'A happy Christmas to everyone, with the usual exception of Norman Whiteside,' was how legendary DJ and Liverpool fan John Peel began his show that night. Little did we suspect at that point that Big Norm, still a folk hero at Old Trafford today, was one of several players in the United dressing room whose days were numbered. Fergie's disciplinarian ways and contempt for past reputations were well known. Gordon Strachan, who'd worked with and then famously fallen out with Ferguson at Aberdeen, had apparently put on a mock display of sobbing, complete with head in hands, when news of his imminent arrival at Old Trafford filtered through to the United dressing room. [1] It was a dressing room packed with members of the now legendary United drinking club and Whiteside was one of its most fervent participants: though he didn't know it at the time, the big Ulsterman's departing handshake wouldn't be far off either.

The game had appeared to have all the hallmarks of a goalless stalemate when he pounced to give United a surprise lead late in the game. Robson's long free kick from his own half was headed down by Stapleton and the ball found its way to Jesper Olsen at the edge of the box. The Dane's simple pass set up Whiteside as he stormed into the area and he thundered his shot into the far corner with customary decisiveness.

Ferguson's decision to release Whiteside less than three years later offered an early glimpse into his uncompromising persona as a manager. Many United fans were predictably appalled by the decision and it said much about Fergie's self-belief that, at a time when dissatisfaction with his reign was at a peak, he was willing to court further animosity with a decision he was clearly knew was the best for the club. It's not as if he regarded Whiteside as a bad player: indeed, he once referred to him as 'close to the genius category' [2] It's the mark of a truly great manager, however, to have the conviction to make decisions that can be unpopular and even baffling to the outside world. Lesser managers will think about them but be put off by the potential repercussions. Fergie was not such a manager.

Fergie himself has admitted that he took too long in making such big decisions, saying he'd hoped to improve the performance of the players he had rather than offload so many clearly very talented footballers. [3]

Some of them – most notably Strachan and Paul McGrath – would go on to enjoy highly successful careers long after their involvement with United was brought to an end. Despite that, it was surely already evident to him that something needed to change. Remarkably, this victory away at the league's best team turned out to be his side's only away win of the season.

A team of undisputed talent was shining all too rarely. Whiteside, a lad from Northern Ireland who crashed into the team as a teenager, had more than a whiff of George Best about him in terms of romance despite being, physically, a very different player. Alex Ferguson, though we didn't know it then, would prove to be a manager willing to sacrifice that romance if it meant building a truly powerful United side in the process.

Liverpool: Grobbelaar, Gillespie, Beglin, Lawrenson, Whelan, Hansen, Dalglish, Venison, Rush, Molby, McMahon.

United: Walsh, Sivebaek, Gibson C., Whiteside, Moran, Duxbury, Robson, Strachan, Stapleton, Davenport, Olsen.

Attendance: 40,663

20 April 1987

Manchester United 1 Liverpool 0

While United's away form during the season was certainly nothing to write home about, at Old Trafford the Reds were undergoing something of a re-surgence, if one that wouldn't be enough to lift us above eleventh place in the league we were heading for that season. Although the enormous satisfaction of that victory at Anfield had quickly dissipated in the wake of a home reverse against Norwich in the next game, since then United had embarked on an unbeaten run of six wins and a single draw at home before welcoming, if that's the right word, our rivals onto our own turf that April.

At the time, Liverpool were involved in a head-to-head tussle with neighbours Everton as they sought to retain the league championship and there was much satisfaction among Reds fans when United inflicted a serious blow to their chances. They wouldn't recover from it and Everton went on to win the league by a nine point margin. Sadly, it was a reflection on United's situation in those days that our rivals' failed attempts to win a trophy were about as good as things got. City's impending relegation would provide an additional reason for celebration that year, while Leeds' failure to win in the play-offs against Charlton also went down pretty well.

In truth, there was little else to get excited about. Following this game, United would go on to win only one further match that season, a meaningless last day encounter against already relegated Aston Villa, and a 4-0 thumping away at Spurs was one of several events which signified that things still hadn't moved forward under Ferguson. No major signings had arrived and there was little at the moment to suggest there was anything special about the new boss's coaching or motivational skills. Indeed, despite the very welcome result of this game, United appeared to spend much of it attempting, often without success, to gauge where that player in the red shirt, who was there a moment ago, had disappeared to. Admittedly the apparent inability to pass to a player on your own team wasn't helped by a heavy wind that that affected both sides.

The season's highest crowd, however, gave predictably loud acclaim to the United goal when it arrived late in the second half. Until then United had enjoyed the bulk of possession but had been thwarted by some acrobatics from Grobbelaar in the Liverpool goal. Eventually, however, the ball fell to Peter Davenport on the edge of the box and the forward struck the winner in front of the Stretford End.

The fun wasn't over for United's fans that day. With the travelling Liverpool support locked inside the ground and news coming through that Everton had beaten Newcastle to take a significant stride towards the championship, many Reds decided to stay behind and taunt them for as long as possible. In those days, you had to enjoy such moments whenever they came along. The truth was, they were far too rare.

United: Walsh, Sivebaek, Moran, Duxbury, McGrath, Gibson, Albiston (Stapleton), Strachan, Moses, Whiteside, Davenport.

Liverpool: Grobbelaar, Venison, Ablett, Hansen, Gillespie, Whelan, Spackman, McMahon, Johnston, Rush, Walsh.

Attendance: 54,103

15 November 1987

Manchester United 1 Liverpool 1

There were signs. It seemed dangerous to do any more than whisper it, but there were signs, even then. Signs that one day soon we might not perhaps be battling Liverpool at the top of the table, but rather meeting them as we went up while they were coming down the other way.

At that point, admittedly, the signs were not exactly vivid. Liverpool would go on to win the league that season with ease and were applauded while doing so from pretty much every quarter for playing the most fluent and imaginative football seen in the English game for years. Even the great Tom Finney hailed one of their performances, a thrashing of Nottingham Forest, as the greatest he'd ever seen. After years of watching Liverpool win everything in sight but comforting ourselves with the knowledge that they we really wouldn't want to be that mind-numbingly dull, we were robbed even of that tiny comfort.

And yet...

Perhaps in Liverpool's newly discovered flamboyance were the seeds of their demise. In the mid-sixties, when Brian Wilson decided he was fed up with making cute surf songs and wanted to be like Dylan and The Beatles and do something more interesting with his time, he was rebuked by his dad/manager and told, apparently pretty forcefully, 'don't fuck with the formula'. Brian did fuck with the formula and it led to the scaling of great new artistic heights as well as, ultimately, mental collapse. The collapse in both cases was somewhat gradual and, at least in Liverpool's case (so far as I'm aware, anyway) didn't involving sitting with your feet in a sandbox, lighting fires in buckets or banging out 'Shortnin' Bread' endlessly on the piano until everyone else got the hell out of the house. However, on reflection, 1987-88 saw Liverpool achieve heights of artistry that even their own fans must have suspected they didn't have in them. At the time the rest of us were inclined to throw our hands up and wonder just how far they could go. They seemed to have moved up to a new level we hadn't even realised was there. Yet it turned out to be a peak that they would never get close to again.

Ferguson had very different issues to contend with, of course. If 1986-87 had shown him anything, it was presumably that United didn't even have a formula to fuck with. Bobby Charlton's concerns prior to his arrival that the United youth system had appeared to dry up was certainly part of the problem. Although important pieces in the jigsaw – such as youth coach Eric Harrison – were already in place, it was clear that many others weren't, and that United's scouting system, which had once famously unearthed talented lads from all over the country, was now barely even deserving of the name.

While it was clear to both Fergie and the board that time would be needed to sort out issues like these, inevitably many United fans were demanding success now. Atkinson's tenure hadn't brought a league championship, but it had brought two FA Cup wins and a series of top four positions. There was a sense at the time that Fergie needed to show he could improve on that and do so very soon – otherwise, popular opinion would conclude he'd only taken the club backwards. If it was unrealistic to hope for a championship yet, United fans did expect far more than the mid-table position of the previous year.

The signs at the start of the season hadn't been hopeful. With those youth and scouting systems taking years to develop, it was clear that Ferguson needed to buy and do so far more effectively than his predecessor had. Yet at that point the only players United had brought in were Brian McClair from Celtic and veteran defender Viv Anderson. Although the purchase of Anderson – by reputation a model professional and non-drinker – made a lot of sense later on, at the time many saw it as a bewildering purchase. McClair's arrival had been greeted more positively: a rare footballer of culture and intellect who was unlikely to be an eagerly sought addition to anyone's boozing club, he'd enjoyed a fantastic scoring record in Scotland and quickly went on to replicate it at United. However, the general feeling was it would take more than this to take United anywhere near to the top of the English game.

By the time the first clash of the season with Liverpool took place, however, there was some cautious optimism. United went into the game having lost only one game that season – to champions Everton – and had even briefly topped the table at the end of August. Although we went into this game in fifth place, we were still very much in the chasing pack behind Liverpool, helped by an autumn goalscoring spell in which McClair had bagged seven in nine games.

Despite United's good form, it had paled in comparison to that of a rampant Liverpool side who'd been pushing aside anything that got in their way with some ease. They were still unbeaten and would remain so until March, at which point the championship was already in the bag. Recent acquisitions Barnes and Beardsley were flying and John Aldridge had got on the scoresheet in each of the first nine games of the season. Although United went into the game with that excellent head to head record behind them, this was clearly going to be a significant test for Ferguson's side. Nevertheless, it was one that, as usual against Liverpool, they managed to rise to.

The ease with which Liverpool opened the scoring hadn't looked too promising for the Reds. Hansen brought the ball out of defence and toyed with the United midfield before lofting a ball forward to McMahon, whose perfect cross found the head of Aldridge and, during that period, such a connection only had one result.

Thankfully Walsh in the United goal somehow managed to deal with a Beardsley shot soon after, or else God knows what might have happened. Liverpool's acquisition of Beardsley had really rubbed United's nose in it. The player stood as a symbol for United's follies in the transfer market during the decade. After a trial with the Reds, Ron Atkinson had opted to let him go after allowing him a single League Cup appearance; since then, after starring at Newcastle, he'd been picked up by Liverpool as a successor to Dalglish on the field and was running riot in the hole behind Aldridge. Beardsley hadn't just been the one who'd got away: he was the one who we'd taken a look at, decided we didn't want and thrown back. And Liverpool were benefitting richly from our inability to spot a decent forward even when we had one in our grasp.

It was again Whiteside, whose days as a thorn in Liverpool's side were of course numbered, who got his side back into the game. After his spectacular scissor kick had been deflected out of play, the resulting corner from Olsen caused problems in the Liverpool box and Kevin Moran muscled the ball into the big man's path for him to add further to his United legend as the best pisser-off of Liverpool fans on the club's books. The opposition's players, strong upholders of the traditional Liverpool FC belief that if anyone had the temerity to score against them there must be something iffy about it, protested to the referee that Moran had used his arm. He probably had. We didn't care.

United: Walsh, Anderson, Moran (Davenport), Gibson, Duxbury, Blackmore, Strachan, Robson, McClair, Whiteside, Olsen.

Liverpool: Grobbelaar, Lawrenson, Nichol, Hansen, Gillespie, McMahon, Whelan, Johnston, Aldridge, Beardsley, Barnes.

Attendance: 47,106

4 April 1988

Liverpool 3 Manchester United 3

The Alex Ferguson/Kenny Dalglish rivalry had history before Fergie even arrived at United. As temporary boss of Scotland following the untimely death of Jock Stein during qualification for the 1986 World Cup, Ferguson had sought the opinions of Dalglish and Hansen on how to deal with the goal threat of their teammate Ian Rush prior to a vital qualifier against Wales. When the players refused to disclose club secrets, Fergie was fuming, accusing them of putting club before country. Although Graeme Souness, by then at Sampdoria, broke ranks with his former colleagues and came to speak with the manager privately about the issue, it was clear that tensions remained and that Fergie had never forgotten what he saw as a betrayal of their homeland. When the World Cup squad for Mexico was announced, Hansen found himself left at home while Dalglish declared himself unfit, with rumours circulating that the real reason was a bust-up with the manager and solidarity with his club captain.

This match, however, remains the key moment in the history of the legendary animosity between the two men. If the infamous pizza fight was the definitive Ferguson-Wenger moment and 'I would love, love it...' was the defining incident of the brief Ferguson-Keegan era, this match and its aftermath showed the world the unbridgeable chasm that existed between the two Scots. It also showed United fans that Ferguson unquestionably got the United-Liverpool rivalry and had a fire in his belly to put one over on them that burned as fiercely as theirs.

With Liverpool already coasting to the league title, the game itself had initially appeared to follow a pattern Dalglish's side had become accustomed to over the season and for a time they looked set to put to bed United's hoodoo over the Anfield outfit of recent years. It didn't turn out like that though and, while even the most ardent United fan could recognise Liverpool's obvious superiority, there was positive evidence of a new character emerging in Ferguson's United.

The game, with Steve Bruce appearing in his first United/Liverpool encounter following his arrival from Norwich, started well for United. In the opening minutes, Peter Davenport cruised into the penalty area on the right, dragging Hansen out of position and finding little resistance from the Liverpool captain when his simple pass inside found Robson unmarked. The captain finished comfortably, but it was the Robson's failure to thwart the run of Hodgson late in the first half that led to Liverpool's equaliser: the Ireland international cruised into the penalty area with time and space to cross for Beardsley, who hammered home.

United had looked the better side up to that point but, following the goal, the home side went up a gear and were in the lead by half-time, a cross from Beardsley leading to a volleyed pass from Barnes towards the head of Gillespie, who nodded into the United goal. Liverpool were two goals in front early in the second half, after a long range finish from McMahon gave Turner no chance, and there was every sign now that the wheels were falling off for United.

It got worse. Colin Gibson was sent off for a second bookable offence. In truth it was the kind of challenge that would warrant that punishment these days, but then would more often than not have resulted in a stern talking-to. The same couldn't be said for Whiteside moments later, who left his foot in on McMahon to receive a booking himself. Though we couldn't be aware of it at the time, it proved a game-changer. Liverpool's decline as a footballing power might not have been in evidence yet, but as it began to set in, one of its features was an increasing tendency among opposing teams, by fair means or foul, to neutralise the midfielder's influence on the field. As Whiteside himself noted: 'I bulldozed McMahon...McMahon, who liked to dish it out but wasn't the greatest guzzler of his own medicine, was wary of me from then on in.' [4]

Against the odds, the ten men began to take control and found themselves back in the contest when Robson's shot from outside the area was helpfully deflected beyond the stranded Grobbelaar. We were soon level. If the nullifying of McMahon would become an important factor in Liverpool's impending decline, another was an increasing lack of dependability in what until then that had been a notoriously efficient back four. That was certainly evident when Davenport produced a peach of a pass to set Strachan through on goal and the United winger finished off before producing remains one of the great iconic United goal celebrations as he mimicked puffing on a cigar, with two pronounced fingers either side of the imaginary object, in front of the Kop.

Despite snatching a daw with ten men from two goals down, Alex Ferguson wasn't happy. Interviewed after the game, he fumed about decisions going against United during the game, including the Gibson sending off, and claimed that managers of other clubs left Anfield, 'choking back the vomit, biting their tongue, afraid to tell the truth.' It was a classic Liverpool-baiting moment from the Scot and arguably the first time United fans really saw the strength of his desire to overcome their rivals. Not only was he willing to put the boot into this much fawned upon Liverpool side (check out the sycophantic commentary from Gerald Sindstadt when the game's highlights were broadcast – tongue firmly down the back of Dalglish's pants) but, crucially, he also took no satisfaction from a draw at the home of the best side in the country. United were heading for second place behind Liverpool in the table that season, a massive improvement on recent years, but Fergie clearly already had his sights on something much higher.

Needless to say, Dalglish didn't react kindly to his comments. He was passing with his baby daughter at the time of the interview and overheard his rival's remarks, intervening to tell the media representatives that they would get more sense out of the toddler.

There would be no defusing of the rivalry between the two in the coming years. United's challenge at the top of the table, however, would prove to be less durable. This was only the fifth time in history that the two clubs had finished first and second in the league and any hope that the Reds would be able to repeat or even reverse the situation in the following season turned out to be hugely over-optimistic.

Liverpool: Grobbelaar, Gillespie, Ablett, Nicol, Spackman, Hansen, Beardsley, Aldridge (Johnston), Houghton, Barnes, McMahon.

United: Turner, Anderson, Blackmore (Olsen), Bruce, McGrath, Duxbury (Whiteside), Robson, Strachan, McClair, Davenport, T Gibson.

Attendance: 43,497

3 September 1988

Liverpool 1 Manchester United 0

If the previous season had hinted that at last United were now moving in a clear upward trajectory under Ferguson, the beginning of the 1988-89 campaign brought us down to earth with a very hefty bump. This first league defeat to Liverpool since 1982 offered further confirmation that we weren't going to be challenging them for the league any time soon. If the draw in April had shown a United side refusing to surrender at the home of their rivals no matter how adverse the circumstances, this offered the reverse: meek capitulation of the most dispiriting kind.

There was an embittered feeling among the Anfield faithful that United's unbeaten run against them had offered United fans an undeserved opportunity at triumphalism. It was, after all, now more than twenty years since the Reds of Manchester had lifted the league championship trophy and the end of the previous campaign had marked twenty years since United's last European triumph. Since then Liverpool had won the European Cup four times and some of them had the temerity to boast that it might have been more, had their colleagues at Heysel not killed those Italian fans and got English clubs banned from Europe. A rather sick claim, you would think, unless you shared the unshakeable belief of many Liverpool supporters that the mass murder had had nothing to do with them, was instead the work of nasty Chelsea supporters who liked nothing better than to drive other supporters to their deaths purely in order to give Liverpool FC a bad name.

They certainly had a point when it came to United's lack of success over the last couple of decades, though, and behind the bravado and pride that goes with being a United fan we knew it all too well. Three FA Cup wins and a second division championship hardly provided convincing boasting material. If anyone expected United fans to tread meekly under the weight of such an ignominious historical burden, however, they had another think coming. No club's fans can rival United's in our determination to use any opportunity whatsoever to demonstrate passionate love for ourclub, which is why, between 1972 and the season just gone, the Reds had consistently enjoyed the biggest home attendances in the league.

The loss of this accolade, to Liverpool of course, did nothing to ease the pressure on Alex Ferguson. Albeit narrowly, Liverpool had added the title of the league's best supported club to all of their other accolades, an average attendance of 39,582 putting them ahead of the Reds' 39,152. Although Anfield's attendance figures had shown a slight improvement, this had more to do with falling crowds at Old Trafford, down by more than a fifth from the previous season. Admittedly, there were mitigating factors. That season, United had introduced a membership scheme, a forerunner of the current scheme but one that was badly administered and generated much bad feeling between club and supporters. Even in the early stages of the season, the club admitted that lost revenue from attendances as a result of the scheme had cost the club around £80,000 in gate revenue. [5] Images of a partly empty Old Trafford certainly did nothing to generate a feel-good factor in these dark times and offered a grim backdrop to what continued to look an unconvincing effort to overcome our rivals, or even sustain a position as their main challengers. Even among those who backed the manager, there was no real sense of conviction that he was the one finally to depose Liverpool and bring back the glory years to United.

Behind the scenes, however, the club continued to make big plans and were already working on an expansion and modernisation of Old Trafford that would bring it in line with the best stadiums in Europe. Meanwhile, Jim Leighton arrived from Fergie's former club Aberdeen while Mark Hughes returned, to great acclaim from the United faithful, from Barcelona. August saw the release of veteran central defender Kevin Moran, a man who had, probably literally, shed more blood for United on the pitch than any other. A further defensive acquisition, the experienced Mal Donaghy, was another very much in the McClair/Anderson mould of solid professionalism, a signing designed, you suspected, to add to the growing number of steadying influences in the United dressing room rather than provide any long-term solutions on the pitch.

This result was one among many in the early stages of the season that dispelled whatever optimism was left over from the previous season. Liverpool pretty much ripped United apart from the off and the only surprise in a first half spent largely in or around our own penalty area was that they only scored one, Steve Bruce's foul on John Barnes leading to a penalty that Jan Molby converted. United at least showed some fight in the second half, with a heated exchange between Robson and Molby and Viv Anderson momentarily leaving his reputation as a gentleman of the game on the sidelines with a crunching two-footed tackle to halt Steve Nicol in full flight. Ultimately though, only a fine save from Leighton and some last ditch defending prevented Liverpool from scoring more.

Liverpool: Grobbelaar, Venison, Nicol, Gillespie, Whelan, Houghton, McMahon (Spackman), Molby, Beardsley, Aldridge (Rush), Barnes.

United: Leighton, Anderson, Bruce, Blackmore, McGrath (Garton), Duxbury, Robson, McClair, Strachan (Davenport), Hughes, Olsen.

Attendance: 42,026

1 January 1989

Manchester United 3 Liverpool 1

If defeat at Liverpool early in the season suggested a distinctly soft underbelly to the Ferguson revolution, this New Year's Day display resonated with at least a temporary glimpse of a more positive future. To give some idea of the changes that had taken place since Fergie's arrival, the thirteen United players involved here included only two (Robson and Strachan) who'd played in Fergie's first United-Liverpool game only a little more than two years ago. Six of the thirteen were playing in the fixture for the first time. By the next game we played Liverpool only Robson would remain from that first encounter.

After spending much of the intervening time around the middle of the table, this victory took United to sixth place and led to a mini-revival of sorts that would see the club reach the optimistic heights of the top three in February, before reality kicked in and the club eventually limped to a dismal tenth place. A new and very unwelcome low was witnessed off the pitch on 2 May when the home game against Wimbledon was watched by a crowd of only 23,368, the lowest Old Trafford attendance for eighteen years.

For now, though, we could at least enjoy this first flight of Fergie's Fledglings. That name has been subsequently attached to the very successful crop of players who emerged in the youth team in the early nineties (now more familiarly known as the Class of 92), but it was with reference to this earlier crop of youngsters that the term was first employed.

With United beset by injuries, several youngsters had been drafted into the first team. Although Lee Sharpe would play a part in the first great Ferguson team of the early nineties and Lee Martin and Mark Robins would have small but significant roles to play in the near future, the majority of those who appeared during this period would eventually leave Old Trafford without making the hoped for impact. Among them was Russell Beardsmore, a diminutive midfielder who received great acclaim for his performance here, pretty much dominating the middle of the park once he'd eased himself into the game and outshining not only illustrious counterparts like Robson and Strachan on his own side, but figures like McMahon in the opposition.

Although Liverpool's assistant manager Ronnie Moran would declare, with audacity laced with the traditional Liverpool helping of sour grapes, that the best team had lost, United fans left Old Trafford that day with a sense that the future might not be so grim as we'd spent much of the season thinking. Many of the personnel would change – with only five of the starting XI here playing a significant part when the new dawn actually arrived – but there was a glimpse here of the kind of blend of youth and experience Fergie was looking for.

It was one of those hundred mile an hour, can't take your eyes of it for a second United/Liverpool clashes. Indeed, in the first half there was probably too much of that, with little time on the ball for either side and a tendency to release the ball rather too quickly either out of a desire to get it up to the other end of the pitch as quickly as possible or to get out of the way of a set of flying studs heading in your direction.

With energy levels beginning to fade, there was more room to exploit in the second half and United looked likely to benefit from it before Liverpool, somewhat against the run of play, struck first. Their goal came in the seventieth minute when Beardsley broke through the middle before releasing Barnes in the area. The winger took a few moments to control the ball before crashing it into the roof of the net with the help of a deflection off the leg of Steve Bruce.

The young heads in United's team might have been forgiven for dropping, but to their great credit the response was positive and swift. There was a gratifying determination about our play in those last twenty minutes, perhaps fuelled by an understandable conviction that this really wasn't a game we deserved to lose. The Reds drew level after Beardsmore's penetrating run into the box had ended with a clever ball to McClair, who scored with a superb scissor-kick. Leighton was called upon to save from McMahon soon afterwards, but from that point it was one way traffic as United hurled bodies forward towards the Stretford End in search of a winner.

McClair's equaliser had had an element of the flamboyance associated with his strike partner Mark Hughes about it and it was now the Welshman's turn to score and put United in front, pouncing on a loose ball following an exchange between Beardsmore and Mark Robins. Then, having had a hand in the first two United goals, Beardsmore deservedly grabbed one himself to clinch the victory, after an excellent by-line cross from Lee Sharpe had found him unmarked in the Liverpool area.

Beardsmore played thirty times for United that season and, for a while, looked to have established himself in the side, especially when

Gordon Strachan moved on in March. In the summer, however, the arrival of Neil Webb and Mike Phelan made it more difficult for the youngster to secure a place in the first team and he was eventually sold to Bournemouth in 1993. He certainly left his mark on this fixture, a match that would arguably go down in history as the one where we finally saw what Fergie was aiming for and understood that it might, eventually, just work.

United: Leighton, Donaghy, Bruce, Martin (McGrath), Beardsmore, McClair, Strachan (Robins), Sharpe, Robson, Hughes, Milne.

Liverpool: Hooper, Staunton (Molby), Burrows, Ablett, Nicol, Whelan, Houghton, McMahon, Aldridge, Barnes, Beardsley.

Attendance: 44,745

23 December 1989

Liverpool 0 Manchester United 0

Despite the optimism generated in the previous match, only the most lavishly optimistic Red would have predicted that this season would end with the Reds' first trophy under Ferguson and far more, if they're honest, were predicting that it would end without Ferguson. The Reds stood a dismal thirteenth in the league at the time of this game and it occurred during an eleven game streak without a win that would leave United entering February in realistic danger of relegation.

That threat was thankfully avoided but, at the time, things looked very bleak indeed. The season had begun with apparent new owner Michael Knighton juggling the ball at the Stretford End prior to kick off and a frankly astonishing demolition of champions Arsenal followed it. Ultimately that result only served to emphasise the rapid decline in what was served up at Old Trafford in the months afterwards.

The hour is darkest, it is said, before dawn. I don't know how true that is but, for now, in terms of United's prospects there seemed only darkness and little prospect of any dawn in sight. The third round of the

FA Cup and that famous goal from Mark Robins that, many claim, was all that stood between Fergie and the sack was still to come. Both Fergie himself and the board have, of course, insisted that there was no question of the manager losing his job at the time and I've nothing to add to that here. All I will say is that few expected the Reds to win that game at Forest and even fewer dared hope that something even better lurked beyond it.

This game ended in a sterile goalless draw, which was large greeted with relief by the suffering Reds faithful, following as it did successive home defeats against Crystal Palace and Spurs. One of few things of note in a generally forgettable game was that Glenn Hysen lined up for his new club against United, having looked poised to sign for us before heading off down the M62 to put pen to paper for Liverpool. Their fans, having obsessively long and very bitter memories where United were concerned, saw it as revenge for us pinching Lou Macari from under their noses in the early seventies.

In the long run, it didn't matter anyway because Hysen turned out to be crap, a player who more than any other would come to symbolise a new defensive frailness that was beginning to set in at Anfield. Meanwhile, although at this point Gary Pallister appeared to have as much difficulty staying on his feet as a baby giraffe, the central defensive partnership he forged with Steve Bruce was actually taking some early steps towards passing into United legend.

Liverpool: Grobbelaar, Venison, Ablett, Hansen (Nicol), Hysen, Houghton, Whelan, McMahon, Molby, Rush, Beardsley.

United: Leighton, Bruce, Pallister, Blackmore, Martin, Robson, Phelan, McClair, Ince, Hughes, Wallace (Sharpe).

Attendance: 37,426

18 March 1990

Manchester United 1 Liverpool 2

The championship trophy Liverpool would be presented with in two months' time remains their last to this day. At the time of this game, that looked about as unlikely as did United challenging for the league title any time soon, something else that turned out to be much closer than any of us dared hope.

The team that capitulated so meekly to Liverpool at home to remain in sixteenth place in the league would, as it turned out, be largely that which, in a few years, would be proclaimed the first great United side for well over two decades. Despite our appalling league position, there were a few glimpses of sunlight peeking through the dark clouds that had been pretty much omnipresent over Old Trafford that season. One had been provided by the win over Sheffield United the previous weekend that had seen the Reds progress to the semi-finals of the FA Cup and a frankly winnable tie against Oldham Athletic. That Liverpool also got through to face a Crystal Palace team they'd demolished 9-0 earlier that season made the prospect of a repeat of the 1977 final a distinct possibility, though few United fans would have sincerely expressed any optimism regarding the prospect of a similar outcome.

But if this soon to be great United side were still pulling off a convincing impression of being crap, the convincing aura Liverpool continued to project would prove to be just as illusory. Indeed, it would be that game against Palace where the mask finally slipped for good as they shipped four goals, surrendering to an aerial bombardment that would leave their defensive vulnerability exposed for all to see and all to exploit in the coming season and beyond. United would then go on to defeat Oldham knowing that only a very beatable Palace side (albeit one that had seen United off at Old Trafford that season) stood between us and some desperately sought after silverware. Needless to say, we didn't make easy work of it. A nervous 3-3 draw would be the score after ninety minutes in both the semi-final and the final before United went on to win both contests after a replay. Mark Robins added to his growing reputation by grabbing an extra time goal to beat Oldham before another youngster, Lee Martin, scored the goal that eventually finished off Palace and brought Ferguson's United that crucial first trophy.

That all seemed very distant now, however, as United fumbled their way to another home defeat. We were shit. Comedy defending allowed John Barnes to break through, the apparent absence of any right side to the United defence allowing him to latch onto Beardsley's simple pass and stroke the ball under Leighton for the opener. The gaps were just as evident when the second goal came in the second half, concerted pressure leading to Rush being upended in the area by Anderson, who was having a nightmare, and allowing Barnes to score his second from the spot.

United were so dismal we even needed Liverpool to score our goal for us. It was a beauty though. Ronnie Whelan grabbed one of the all-time great own goals when his inexplicable inch-perfect lob left Grobbelaar scrambling forlornly to allow the Reds an unlikely route back into the game. Unfortunately, at that time, we were still in the habit of looking gift horses like that one in the mouth and Liverpool proceeded to secure the win without much effort. United's resistance on the day had been so weak, it was unlikely the visitors even needed a post-match shower.

United: Leighton, Anderson (Duxbury), Bruce, Pallister, Blackmore, Martin, McClair, Phelan, Ince, Wallace (Beardsmore), Hughes.

Liverpool: Grobbelaar, Venison, Staunton, Hansen, Hysen, Houghton, Whelan, McMahon, Barnes, Beardsley, Rush.

Attendance: 46,629

18 August 1990

FA Charity Shield

Wembley

Liverpool 1 Manchester United 1

United's return to Wembley after that FA Cup triumph was their first appearance in the Charity Shield since 1985 and their first appearance against Liverpool in this game since 1983, when the Reds had run out winners.

Here, United took the lead just before half-time. Mike Phelan's cross into the box was completely missed by Mark Hughes but the ball fell to Clayton Blackmore at the far post, who instinctively prodded home. Liverpool equalised in the second half after Pallister's challenge on Barnes resulted in the customary penalty for the Anfield side, even though there was no doubt Pally got the ball. The Liverpool player's Brian Phelps impersonation, together with the yellow card Paul Ince received for his heated protests following the incident, said much about how both sides were treating this game as far more than just a glorified pre-season friendly, as it would become for United in later years.

Barnes took and scored the penalty himself. Blackmore came close to securing victory for United when, following a foul on Ince on the edge of the area, his shot from a free kick was clawed away by Grobbelaar. The same player also found the Liverpool keeper in the way when his acrobatic volley was kept out in the closing minutes of the game. Although honours finished even, there was no question that United finished the stronger, providing much optimism for the season ahead and indeed for the game at Anfield the following month.

Having said that, you might want to skip this next one...

Liverpool: Grobbelaar, Hysen, Burrows, Venison, Whelan, Ablett, Beardsley (Rosenthal), Houghton, Rush, Barnes, McMahon.

United: Sealey, Irwin, Donaghy, Bruce, Phelan, Pallister, Blackmore, Ince, McClair, Hughes, Wallace (Robins).

Attendance: 66,558

16 September 1990

Liverpool 4 Manchester United 0

The end of Liverpool's reign at the top didn't seem too imminent here, where Fergie, having finally broken his trophy duck with United, saw his side ravished by a side who clearly wished to put us very firmly in our places in a manner that, in truth, they'd rarely managed to do in recent times. Indeed, this was the most serious stuffing they'd administered to us since a 5-0 thrashing back in 1925.

Salt was duly rubbed into the freshly opened wound when Beardsley, that symbol of United's early eighties transfer follies, grabbed a hat trick. On this evidence, it was very difficult to say whether the alleged weaknesses in Liverpool's back four had any substance because we barely tested them.

Let's move on…

Liverpool: Grobbelaar, Burrows, Nicol, Gillespie, Hysen, McMahon, Houghton, Whelan, Rush, Beardsley, Barnes.

United: Sealey, Bruce, Pallister (Donaghy), Irwin, Blackmore, Ince (Beardsmore), Phelan, Webb, McClair, Hughes, Robins.

Attendance: 35,726

31 October 1990

Rumbelows League Cup 3rd Round

Manchester United 3 Liverpool 1

Thankfully, it wasn't long before United got the opportunity to test that Liverpool defence properly and put that previous nightmare behind us. We did so magnificently: the headline in The Times the following morning read 'United Dismantle Liverpool Aura of Invincibility', reflecting the emerging realisation that Liverpool's long period of dominance in English football might well be coming to an end, [6] while The Guardian's headline indicated where the Achilles heel had finally been located: 'United Expose Liverpool Rearguard' it read. [7]

The Times continued, 'United did not merely win. They were in complete control…Everything on the pitch fizzled, everything on the terraces crackled.' The Guardian, while noting that this was Liverpool's first defeat since the loss to Crystal Palace in the FA Cup, also pointed out that many of the same defensive weaknesses were in evidence here, also noting that the eventual margin of victory for United might have been even greater had David Burrows been dismissed for his foul on Danny Wallace, a punishment the offence had clearly deserved.

To say there was a new fighting spirit about United was putting it mildly and also had something of a literal ring about it at the time. This match followed hard on the heels of the infamous brawl against Arsenal that led to both teams receiving points deductions. Here, they took the fight to Liverpool in a purely footballing sense, however, and it was hard to recognise the United side here from the one that surrendered so spiritlessly at Anfield a month earlier.

Grobbelaar's erratic performance was another factor in United's dominance. Early on he failed to deal with a Lee Sharpe cross despite being completely unchallenged. McClair failed to capitalise on the loose ball but the series of corners that followed emphasised Liverpool's vulnerability at the back. United soon exploited it. Irwin, still in his original incarnation as a right back, floated a cross into the box and, with Grobbelaar flapping wildly at nothing, Nicol handled to prevent Steve Bruce from getting a header in at the far post. Bruce himself stepped up to give United the lead from the spot.

The second goal, which came less than a minute later, was a stunner. Mark Hughes battled his way through the Liverpool midfield and defence before thrashing a thunderbolt past Grobbelaar. With Ince dominating the midfield and Bruce snuffing out the threat of Ian Rush at the back, United were close to imperious and this continued into the second half. Although there was a brief wake-up call when Rush, left completely unmarked, spooned a chance over the bar, it remained largely one way traffic and it was no surprise when United added a third with nine minutes left. Grobbelaar was once again at fault, tamely pawing a header from Pallister back into play and finding Sharpe, who hammered the ball back past the keeper.

'Serious questions had to be raised about Grobbelaar's goalkeeping,' The Guardian remarked. These words would turn out to be far more prescient than the newspaper could have anticipated: just four years later he was caught in a sting by The Sun, having been videotaped discussing his role in fixing matches. He was, let me be clear, entirely NOT GUILTY, even though the judge would remark that he had 'acted in a way in which no decent or honest footballer would act.' Many Liverpool fans I know continue to claim the video was a fake, even though Grobbelaar didn't make any such claim in his defence. I know several United fans whose minds went back to this match when the claims broke. And understandably so because, even though he was clearly NOT GUILTY, I've never in all my years witnessed such a bizarre and eccentric goalkeeping display at Old Trafford, and that includes Paddy Roche.

Houghton's deflected shot pulled one back for Liverpool, but the game was already lost and United progressed into the fourth round where we would pull off an even more stunning victory by hammering eventual league champions Arsenal 6-2. Although the Reds' League Cup campaign would end in disappointment with defeat in the final to Sheffield Wednesday, these two wins against the two best clubs in England were huge statements by Ferguson's side, illustrating that, on their day, his United were a match for anyone. He simply needed to get those days to happen more often.

The day after that Arsenal win an event occurred that was yet another step towards bringing that about: a young lad called Ryan Giggs signed a senior contract with the club.

United: Sealey, Bruce, Pallister, Irwin, Blackmore, Phelan (Donaghy), Webb, McClair, Ince, Sharpe, Hughes (Wallace).

Liverpool: Grobbelaar, Nicol, Burrows (Rosenthal), Staunton, Gillespie, Hysen, Molby, Houghton, McMahon, Rush, Beardsley.

Attendance: 42,033

3 February 1991

Manchester United 1 Liverpool 1

If you were looking retrospectively for clues regarding the shift in the balance of power that was about the take place in English football, there were plenty in this game and the events that followed soon after. David Speedie, a player whose signing indicated more than any other that Liverpool had by now completely lost the plot in the transfer market, took the field for his first United v Liverpool game. Dalgish's signing of Speedie alongside that of Jimmy Carter from Millwall left even many Liverpool fans scratching their heads. The manager who had once made the double swoop that brought Beardsley and Barnes to Anfield, and the club that had founded much of its success on intelligence in the transfer market, appeared to be squandering good money on players who were, in the much-repeated words of much of the media of the period, generally agreed to be 'not Liverpool standard'.

There were clear signs that Dalglish was struggling. Clearly he'd been greatly, and understandably, affected by the events at Hillsborough almost two years earlier. There'll be more about Hillsborough later on in this book but at this stage I'll simply state that I've no time for those in the United support who fail to show respect for one of the most horrifying events in modern football history. Not do I find any less despicable those Liverpool supporters who've alleged an anti-Hillsborough sentiment in my online articles down the years: frankly, none but the most twisted individual could ever detect such a thing. I'll certainly document any instances of the negative behaviour of Liverpool and their fans in this book. However, it surely can't be difficult for anyone to understand that the club on this occasion suffered the most appalling tragedy as well as being on the wrong end of a despicable cover up and a series of outrageous lies in its aftermath.

In addition to the disaster's impact on Dalglish, there were already suggestions that the legendary fabric of the club's Boot Room culture was coming apart. For the first two years of his tenure, Dalglish had wisely drawn upon the services of legendary former manager Bob Paisley for guidance. Now, he was making decisions on his own and many of them looked decidedly questionable. Just nineteen days after this game, the Liverpool boss would shock the football world by announcing his resignation.

The significance of this decision in the story of the decline of his club can't be underestimated. Even since Bill Shankly's arrival in 1959, the club had not only promoted managerial successors from within, but planned that succession as carefully as the club planned everything during its period of dominance. Now, a manager had quit them mid-season and clearly the club was as stunned by the news as anyone else. This time there was no obvious replacement and no obvious succession strategy. For the first time in the modern era they found themselves overtaken by events. In many respects, they still haven't recovered.

On an absolute shit heap of an Old Trafford pitch, United took the lead in much the same manner as we had in the previous meeting. An apparently harmless corner was floated into the box and Glenn Hysen inexplicably put his hand up to it, giving the referee an easy decision to make. Hysen sat in the mud, appearing to suggest that even he struggled to understand what he'd just done. So clear was the offence that even his Liverpool team mates, then as now much given to histrionic displays of outrage whenever anything doesn't go their way, didn't even protest the decision. Brucey duly stepped up to score his seventh penalty of the season and his second against Liverpool.

The visitors responded quickly. Barnes left four United defenders in his wake to get free on the left and deliver a bewitching cross into the box that Sealey could only get the smallest of touches to; Speedie, in a moment that bought him some time among those many Liverpool fans unconvinced by his arrival, pounced to equalise.

United took the game to our opponents in the second half and, for the second match running in this fixture, Liverpool ought to have been down to ten men when Grobbelaar deliberately handled outside the box. Again, the visitors got away with a yellow card. Once again, it seemed that nothing short of buggering a United player at knife point was going to lead to a sending off for anyone in a Liverpool kit.

The game duly trundled to a draw, a third successive one in Liverpool's case, vital points lost in their efforts to finish ahead of Arsenal in the league and a missed opportunity to capitalise on the Gunners' first – and, as it would turn out,, only – defeat in the league at Chelsea a day earlier. When, within a fortnight of Dalglish's departure, Arsenal won at Anfield it made their task even harder and George Graham's side duly went on to win the league despite the two point penalty that had followed those fisticuffs at Old Trafford.

For United, the best was to come. Although the disappointment of defeat in the League Cup Final was still to be endured, and the club limped to a poor sixth place in the league, a series of, let's face it, pretty straightforward ties in the European Cup Winners' Cup led the Reds to a first European final for 23 years. We'd be given little chance in Rotterdam, facing a Barcelona side with the likes of Ronald Koeman and Michael Laudrup in their ranks, but on a memorable night a 2-1 victory allowed United fans a first taste of European success since that famous European Cup triumph under Matt Busby. It was also the first time since that night that a United side had won major trophies in successive seasons. And of course the great thing was, it turned out we'd only just got started.

United: Sealey, Pallister, Bruce, Irwin, Blackmore, McClair, Robson, Phelan (Martin), Webb (Wallace), Sharpe, Hughes.

Liverpool: Grobbelaar, Staunton, Ablett, Nicol, Burrows, Hysen, McMahon (Molby), Whelan, Barnes, Speedie, Rush.

Attendance: 43,690

Performance records

(First Ferguson v Dalglish period)

Played – 12
United wins -4
Draws – 5
Liverpool wins – 3
United goals – 15
Liverpool goals - 15

Honours

United – 1 FA Cup; 1 FA Charity Shield (shared).
Liverpool – 2 League Championships; 1 FA Cup; 3 FA Charity Shields (including one shared)

Transfer expenditure

Incoming transfers
United – £14.69 million
Liverpool – £11.96 million

Outgoing transfers
United – £6.04 million
Liverpool – £6.42 million

Net spend
United – £8.65 million
Liverpool - £5.54 million

References:
1. L. Moynihan, Gordon Strachan
2. N. Whiteside, Whiteside, p265
3. A. Ferguson, Leading, pp88-89
4. **www.whitesideone.com/2014/03/liverpool-3-3-manchester-united-april.html**
5. M. Crick & D Smith, Manchester United – The Betrayal of a Legend, p134
6. The Times, 1 November 1990
7. The Guardian, 1 November 1990

2

Seizing the Perch

Ferguson v Souness

6 October 1991

Manchester United 0 Liverpool 0

So often in the past it had been United going through painful and difficult transition periods while Liverpool remained their steady, efficient selves. The tables had turned dramatically. On the tenth anniversary of Bryan Robson's arrival at the club, Liverpool turned up looking anything like that team of old. Their former captain Graeme Souness was now installed as manager. It had, apparently, been the next best thing to an appointment from within, but already things weren't going well: they'd won only four of their first nine league games and would only win a further three before Christmas. By then, they'd also endured the rare humiliation of a League Cup defeat at mighty Peterborough.

Souness had rung the changes in the transfer market and been given the funds to do so, but the acquisitions had a look of anxious desperation about them, far more reminiscent of Atkinson-era United than the kind of cautiously planned evolution that had been the hallmark of Liverpool during their glory years. They'd splurged a British record transfer fee on Dean Saunders, while the signing of Mark Wright would prove to be just one of a succession of changes designed to plug gaps in a leaky central defence clearly still suffering from the failure to plan effectively for the retirement of Hansen. Mark Walters looked a similarly unimpressive capture, while the departure of David Speedie after only a few months at the club emphasised that transfer market follies weren't something Souness had brought to the club on his own. Those who took part here included six for whom a United-Liverpool clash was a new experience, the largest number of fixture debutants to take the field for Liverpool during Fergie's reign at Old Trafford.

Among a Liverpool support that largely refused to accept any criticism of Dalglish, Souness would soon be designated official scapegoat for the club's decline. In truth all he'd been guilty of was poor plugging of the holes in a ship that had looked bound to sink long before he got on it. That it coincided with a United side winning trophies for the first time in years made the situation even more difficult to swallow for those fans and made Souness' position still more tenuous. Many, including future Liverpool favourite Jamie Carragher, have correctly pointed out that, despite that determination to 'knock Liverpool off their perch', there was actually no point at which a power tussle between the two sides took place at the top: if anyone removed Liverpool from the pinnacle of the English game, it had been Arsenal, with United at this point simply poising themselves to move into the empty space vacated by both. However, there is little doubt that United's rise at the time put extra pressure on Liverpool's manager and board and may well have helped to nudge them into the poor planning and desperation in the transfer market that ensured this was far more than just a temporary lapse.

Despite that, and against all evidence to the contrary, many media pundits had predicted a quick return to the top for Liverpool this season, a number of newspaper commentators tipping the club to win the league, bolstered by their transfer market activity and a manager who, after all, had already achieved much with Rangers north of the border. Remembering how Ferguson had been regarded as inevitably out of his depth when moving down from Scotland to England, the irony of the comments won't have been lost on many United fans.

The Reds, in contrast, had been quiet in the transfer market during the summer, swooping only to pick up right back Paul Parker – a move that would allow Denis Irwin to switch to left back, a position in which he would perhaps only be rivalled by Patrice Evra as United's best ever – and a relatively unknown goalkeeper from Brondby called Peter Schmeichel, signed for a mere £550,000. Although there had been some edgy moments early on, Schmeichel soon slotted in behind a tight defence that had conceded only three goals in ten games: it was United's best start to a season since 1985 and the Reds were top of the league and unbeaten going into this game, three points ahead and with two games in hand of nearest challengers Leeds while Liverpool struggled in 13th place.

While Liverpool were making much of youthful prodigies Steve McManaman and Mike Marsh along with the acquisition of nineteen-year-old Rob Jones from Crewe, there were emerging rumours of a very special number of teenage prospects coming through United's academy. In the first team already was the leader of the charge, Ryan Giggs, a nailed-on certainly for PFA Young Player of the Year even at that early stage of the season. Giggs had made his United debut the previous spring and would, of course, still be a part of the United squad when Alex Ferguson reached the end of his management career. Thankfully, both of those situations were still some way off. There would be a hell of a lot of history to make between now and then.

Not today, though. As the scoreline suggests, this was a largely forgettable game. Although a Red & White Kop participant some years later would recall 'Rob Jones keeping Ryan Giggs in his pocket' on that day as a highlight of his life (!), it was, in truth, more a case of so much physical play and so many heated exchanges that no one on either side got the chance to play much football, Graeme Souness having very much stamped his own highly physical character on his team while Fergie's new United side weren't exactly shrinking violets either. In the event, the game was most notable for a couple of sendings off. Yes, remarkably a Liverpool player was dismissed at Old Trafford, Gary Ablett receiving two yellows for taking Blackmore roughly from behind, so to speak, and a reckless trip on Andrei Kanchelskis that ended the Ukrainian's involvement in the game before half-time. Mark Hughes received his marching orders after a tussle with David Burrows ended with the Welshman throwing his head in the direction of the Liverpool defender. It was that kind of game.

United: Schmeichel, Phelan (Kanchelskis), Irwin, Bruce, Blackmore, Pallister, Robson, Ince (Donaghy), McClair, Hughes, Giggs.

Liverpool: Hooper, Ablett, Nicol, Burrows, Jones (Marsh), Tanner, McMahon, Houghton, Saunders (McManaman), Walters, Rush.

Attendance: 44,997

26 April 1992

Liverpool 2 Manchester United 0

It never felt worse than this. What we know now was that this failed tilt at the title was but the first in a series of such tilts. It felt then like a failure to secure the league title for the first time in 25 years and that it might be another 25 before we got another shot at it. And to lose it to Leeds and at Anfield of all places...

Younger Reds, be thankful you were not born to witness such a day. Take the loss to city in the last moments of the 2011-12 season and times it by a hundred and you still wouldn't get close to understanding how much this one hurt. United had looked champions elect all season only to begin spluttering in the spring while a frankly ordinary-looking Leeds side marshalled brilliantly by former Red Gordon Strachan, who was clearly relishing the opportunity to put one over a former boss with whom his disputes were the stuff of legend, simply refused to go away.

With only occasional interruptions, United had led the league until six days before this game. A victorious campaign in the League Cup culminating in the defeat of Nottingham Forest at Wembley had led to a fixture backlog and a punishing schedule that saw the Reds having to play five games in ten days at the end of the season: indeed, many would speculate that, had United lost to Leeds when the two sides had met in the competition back in January, it might well have been their rivals who'd be struggling to cope with the pile-up and...well, we'd spend all summer mulling over such hypotheticals.

The Reds had seen off Southampton at home before a disappointing draw at Luton, which had still left us at the top of the table with four games of the league season to go. Then the wheels fell off. Forest came to Old Trafford and gained revenge for the League Cup Final defeat, a home reverse that handed the initiative and the league leadership to Leeds. Defeat at West Ham two days later gift-wrapped that initiative and presented it to them with chocolates and flowers. Two Sunday fixtures followed: if Leeds beat Sheffield United in the earlier game, it left the Reds needing at least a draw at Liverpool, and realistically a win, to stand any chance of winning the league. Leeds beat Sheffield United.

Predictably, United arrived at Anfield with the Kop in extremely good spirits. Although this had been Liverpool's worst season in the league since before Bob Paisley took over, they'd somehow found themselves in the FA Cup Final and inevitably drew extra delight from our unanticipated stumbling over those final hurdles. As their side moved towards victory over a United side that looked frankly knackered and with the fighting spirit that had been such a feature of the campaign completely drained out of them, the chants of 'You'll never win the league' and 'You lost the league on Merseyside' reached volume levels not heard at Anfield for years and United's response was simply to wilt further. Rush opened the scoring for Liverpool early in the first half – remarkably, his first ever goal against United – and there was clearly no way back for the Reds long before Mark Walters added a second three minutes before time.

In retrospect this game marked the start of a new stage of the rivalry between the two sides. The forthcoming FA Cup final, which Liverpool won, would only serve to paper over the cracks for a club clearly heading in a downward direction. Cheering on Leeds to this title would mark the beginning of a phase in which their fans would be continually condemned to seek victory by proxy, essentially cheering for anyone who was playing us and feeding off the rare crumbs of failure that fell from the feast that was soon to be enjoyed by United fans.

It didn't feel that way at the time, but the game marked a complete reversal in the nature of the rivalry between the two clubs: in the recent past, United fans had supported Arsenal, or anyone else who might be making a challenge to Anfield's dominance in the hope that, if we didn't win anything ourselves, at least they could stop Liverpool rubbing in the misery by adding more trophies to their bulging cabinet. From this point, it would be Liverpool fans who would be forced to endure season after season of meagre success, if any at all, while clinging to the hope that at least United might be occasionally denied it.

Had we known that this would merely be a last faltering step prior to the great years truly returning to United, it would of course been far easier to take. Instead, the chants from the Kop and the words of so many football commentators and 'experts' judged us, perhaps understandably, on a history of previous campaigns that had fizzled out, this one having simply taken longer to do so. 'An alehouse team who will never win the league' was the verdict of one gloating letter-writer to the Liverpool Daily Post. Chances for United to win the league didn't come around very often, went the conventional wisdom of the time, and when one had we'd been found painfully wanting.

What neither we nor they could have known was that this time it would be very different. This was now a very different United, led by a manager and a whole group of players who had the character not to allow a setback like to deflect them from their professional goals. Among the many words written about our failure to win the league, it went unremarked upon that the Reds had, with the League Cup, now won a trophy for three seasons running. Small consolation for what followed, admittedly. But it did show that this was now a team of winners, a group of individuals who would approach season 1993-94 using the pain of this moment as fuel for a fire raging in their bellies that neither Liverpool nor anybody else would be able to put out.

Liverpool: Hooper, Jones, Wright, Burrows, Tanner (Venison), Thomas, Houghton, Molby, Saunders, Barnes, Rush (Walters).

United: Schmeichel, Donaghy, Pallister (Phelan), Bruce, Irwin, McClair, Robson, Giggs, Ince, Kanchelskis, Hughes.

Attendance: 38,669

18 October 1992

Manchester United 2 Liverpool 2

Liverpool fans were still buzzing after United's failure in the previous season when this first United-Liverpool game of the new Premier League took place. We'd started the season badly, losing the first two games with performances that appeared to justify the views of those doubters who'd argued we'd shot our bolt last season and wouldn't get an opportunity like that again anytime soon. Although we'd bounced back from that poor start with a run of five victories, we'd followed those with three draws, including a deeply unconvincing 0-0 against QPR, which left us in fifth place before this game. When November came around, an extremely weak performance and defeat at Aston Villa would leave the Reds tenth. In short, at the time this looked anything like the season that would end United's long wait for a league title.

Liverpool supporters entering Old Trafford that day were happily nursing a similar conviction. Not only were United stumbling in the league, we'd fallen at the first hurdle in the UEFA Cup, losing on penalties to Torpedo Moscow. Liverpool fans could be entirely satisfied that, although their own team certainly weren't looking any great shakes at the moment, their rivals from the other end of the East Lancs Road appeared to have seen their upward momentum of the last three seasons come to an abrupt halt. The weird look to the Stretford End appeared at the time a suitable backdrop, the terraces standing vacant as the transition to all-seater stadia across the country continued. Incidentally, you might want to take this into account before regarding the attendance figure for this game as a misprint. Due to the closure of a quarter of the ground, this would turn out to be, to date, the last year in which United's average home attendance was outstripped by that of Liverpool.

What those Liverpool fans didn't realise, of course, was that they'd already had a glimpse of the future when, in the Charity Shield, a certain Eric Cantona had struck a fine hat trick for Leeds. Although neither we nor they were aware of it at the time, future Liverpool boss and then French national manager Gerard Houllier was already manoeuvring behind the scenes to get Cantona to United, concerned at how Leeds were utilizing, or rather under-utilizing, his star player. [1]

But the results of those manoeuvres were, at the time, merely the stuff of speculation, if that. United fans were simply aware that, for all the many positive features of the current squad, something was still missing to bring out the very best from this group of players. I'm sure, if they're honest, almost all United fans would admit that they didn't see the answer to that problem anywhere in the Leeds squad, still less that Leeds would present it to us for a bargain fee.

The consolation, of course, was that Liverpool looked even less convincing. This eleven contained only five players from the side that had won the league in 1990 and, while many at Anfield deluded themselves that the likes of Mike Marsh, Don Hutchison and Torben Piechnik would eventually step up and fill the shoes of former legends, they were certainly showing no sign of it at the moment.

Manager Souness had returned following a heart operation towards the end of the previous season. However, despite that FA Cup win, his position had not been made easier during his enforced absence due to a well-publicised fall-out with reserve team manager Phil Thompson. There had been rumours of animosity between the two men that went back to their playing days but, when Thompson openly criticized his manager in earshot of Alex Ferguson and Brian Kidd, no less, the Liverpool boss felt he had no option but to dismiss him. [2] It was the kind of decision that went with the job but the loss of Thompson from the club's staff looked to many of the fans like just another example of a respected and loyal club servant leaving the club.

On the pitch, a blatant dive from Hutchison when challenged by Steve Bruce early in the game confirmed that some things didn't change. United's best chances early on both fell to Darren Ferguson, the manager's son. The opportunities were duly spurned: indeed, he'd have got no less weight behind the two shots had he waved his dick at them. It was, it had to be said, fitful stuff from United, although it was still something of a shock when we went behind, Hutchison's speculative effort taking a heavy deflection off Bruce to squirm past Schmeichel.

United's main threat was coming from the wings but, with Ferguson's plans to sign Mick Harford thankfully shelved, there was little chance of any United player without a set of stepladders getting to the crosses that Kanchelskis, in particular, was providing. Although Liverpool's efforts on goal had mainly tested the ball boys whose task it was to retrieve the results of their misfired shots from the vacant Stretford End, United had only themselves to blame when we conceded a second. Rush, having famously never scored against United until that terrible day in April, doubled his tally here after putting away Rosenthal's cut-back from the line a minute before half-time. The goal also saw Rush pass Roger Hunt's long-standing goalscoring record for the club.

Alex Ferguson's half-time rants had already attained legendary status and you can only imagine what he had to say here, 2-0 down at half-time to a Liverpool side so bad the goals appeared to come as more of a surprise to them than their opponents. Whatever he said, something changed in the second half as United attacked with much greater purpose.

It was late when United finally got back into the game, but it was done with style, Hughes drifting into the box to latch onto a long pass and looping a volley over Grobbelaar with only twelve minutes left on the clock. The Reds threw everything into attack in pursuit of an equaliser that, with Liverpool looking increasingly fraught at the back, always seemed likely to come. When it did, it was another cracker, Giggs' cross from the left met by Hughes' bullet header at the near post.

Fergie, who'd characteristically been kicking out at every ball on the bench, raced down to chide his players for celebrating the goal: although the game was entering stoppage time, he clearly felt there was time for a winner.   After the game, however, he admitted his side probably hadn't even deserved a point.   The fight back said much about the evolving spirit of that United side, although the fact that we'd let the game drift so badly in the first place and had to settle for a draw illustrated once again that a vital piece was still missing.   Although we didn't know it at the time, that weekend it was trooping off the pitch at Elland Road to be replaced by Carl Shutt.

United: Schmeichel, Parker, Bruce, Pallister, Irwin, Kanchelskis (Blackmore), Ince, Giggs, McClair, Ferguson, Hughes.

Liverpool: Grobbelaar, Burrows, Nicol, Piechnik, Marsh, Molby (Tanner), Hutchison, McManaman, Redknapp (Thomas), Rush, Rosenthal.

Attendance: 33,243

6 March 1993

Liverpool 1 Manchester United 2

If Liverpool fans thought they'd be coming to watch United in the process of blowing the league as they had in the equivalent fixture last year, they were to be seriously disappointed. It wasn't clear yet that we wouldn't mess it up again, of course, but this victory lanced a particularly irritating boil that had persisted since April the previous year and exorcised some important demons in the process. What was also clear by now, as hadn't been the case last year, was that the idea of United fighting for league titles was something we might expect to become familiar with, while Liverpool were continuing to head in the other direction, with knobs on.

United went into this game top of the league, and although there were a few hiccups to come after this game (defeat to Oldham followed three consecutive draws), we'd go on to secure the championship at a canter, winning the last seven games and finishing ten points clear of closest challengers Aston Villa. We were, in short, a team transformed from the one that had snatched an unconvincing draw against these opponents earlier in the season and, although there was no one reason for that there was one that stood well above all the others and you already know what that is.   Indeed, since that Villa defeat that took us down to tenth place we'd been unbeaten and this win would extend that run to sixteen games. Eric Cantona had made his debut in the third game of that run.

More will inevitably be said about the mercurial Frenchman in the pages to come. For now, let's simply note that he slipped effortlessly into this United team, not just imbuing it with his unique skills but galvanising all that was around him. He was also cocky as hell. Fergie has noted that, when first arriving at Old Trafford he wasn't, as so many top class players are, overawed by his surroundings, but instead seemed to be sizing them up, assessing whether or not the club was big enough for him. Former Liverpool captain Alan Hansen, by now working for the BBC, was dismissive of Cantona's attributes on his arrival at United, regarding him as a luxury player with a lot of fancy touches but nothing special.   His predecessor Emlyn Hughes labeled Cantona 'a flashy foreigner' [3] while former Leeds captain Billy Bremner reckoned it would have been a far worse blow to his former club had they lost David Batty or Gary Speed. [4] It was a commonly held view at the time and presumably one of the reasons why Leeds had allowed him to leave to deadly rivals for only a little over a third of what Liverpool had paid for Dean Saunders.

Cantona was also regarded, to put it mildly, as a difficult character. He'd only arrived in Britain as a result of his being banned in France. After Sheffield Wednesday had passed on an option to sign him, Leeds had snapped him up but, although he'd given them something different, he was largely regarded as a bit-part player in the side that had won the championship. United, despite the comments of Hansen and others, were prepared to let him take centre stage, and to say he flourished would be the understatement of the decade or any other decade.

Cantona was missing from this game but any hopes among the Liverpool faithful that United would struggle without him were soon put to bed.   Hughes rose majestically to open the scoring with a brilliant header and, although substitute Rush grabbed his third goal in three against United to equalise with an impressive volley in the second half, United ran out deserving winners when McClair popped up in the box six minutes later to head home from a corner.

Despite United's dominance, the result might have been in doubt had Schmeichel not pulled off a frankly impossible looking save from Hutchison in the first half. It was a reminder, if any were needed, that much as Cantona received deserved plaudits for bringing United's attacking play to life, the Danish goalie already looked just as important at the other end of the pitch. That the two of them jointly cost less than Liverpool were regularly shelling out for journeyman defenders spoke volumes about United's transfer policy and, in Schmeichel's case, the scouting network that had been revitalised under Ferguson. They were two of a group of players Fergie later referred to as 'six absolute warriors' [5] in his squad back then – the other four being Bruce, Ince, Robson and Hughes – who'd imbued the dressing room with a winning spirit that simply made it unthinkable that they'd let the disappointment of last year blow them off course.

Needless to say, all memories of the previous season's disappointment were now forgotten as the Reds were presented with the championship trophy at the end of the season after a gap of 26 years, following a game against Blackburn that had been rendered meaningless by Villa's defeats against Blackburn and Oldham. Liverpool once again finished in sixth place, with this game one of 15 defeats over the season, the highest number they'd suffered since 1964-65. United had been champions that year too.

Liverpool: James, Wright, Bjornabye, Nicol, Jones, McManaman, Hutchison, Redknapp, Stewart (Rush), Walters (Burrows), Barnes.

United: Schmeichel, Parker, Pallister, Bruce, Irwin, Sharpe, Ince, Kanchelskis, McClair, Giggs, Hughes.

Attendance: 44,374

4 January 1994

Liverpool 3 Manchester United 3

'Liverpool will be back next year,' had been an often heard prediction over the previous couple of years, emanating from both within the club's support and wider media circles. Looking back, it was revealing that, at the start of the 1992/93 season, Liverpool had been 7/2 second favourites with the bookmakers behind Arsenal, with United quoted at a distant 4/1. [6] From a historical perspective, it's hard to see what such a forecast could have been based on, apart from blind faith and the belief nurtured over many years that you wrote the club off at your peril. Now it's hard to understand how anyone could have failed to see the signs of decline that had set in. Increasingly desperate plunges into the transfer market and a faith, against all evidence, that last season's mediocrities would somehow emerge as world-beaters in the next were not the hallmarks of a club following a clearly defined and well thought out strategy, let alone those of potential champions.

So it was no surprise to the rest of us that things continued to get worse. Souness had used this year's transfer budget to sign a couple of players very much in his own hard man image, bringing serial red card recipient Julian Dicks and Neil 'Razor' Ruddock to the club over the summer, balancing that with the more subtle skills of Nigel Clough who, to put it mildly, had about as much aggression in his performances as the average Morris Dancer.

As the balance of power shifted significantly in the direction of Old Trafford, Liverpool fans nowabandoned almost overnight their allegations, built up during an almost permanently aggrieved tantrum in years when they should really have been enjoying themselves, that United weren't even really a big club, but one built up to be such by a friendly media. Now, they moaned that United's spending power was giving them an unfair advantage in the transfer market that just wasn't fair. They clung to the image of their own club as a cute, piglet-y homely collection of individuals trying to do things the right way in the nasty commercial world. The 'Liverpool way', they claimed, was built on home grown talent and the nurturing of good honest lads into teams that, through collective effort and those special red shirts, would take on the world.

These were, to put it mildly, utterly bogus claims. Although United had invested heavily in the squad in the late eighties, by now Alex Ferguson's far more frugal and cautious approach was prevailing. He favoured 'value in the market', making occasional high profile signings when the right player became available – Roy Keane, who'd arrived in the summer, was such a player – but elsewhere making less sizeable amounts go an extremely long way to bring in players like Schmeichel, Cantona and Irwin, all of whom were playing like big name transfers, but collectively had cost the club less than Liverpool had spent on Ruddock alone.

During Souness' time at the club, Liverpool's transfer spending would easily exceed that of United and, although they recouped some of this through the sale of members of the squad he inherited, few of the players he bought would turn out to be worth the investment. Although United would move out of this surplus in the late nineties, this would be made possible by a firmly established wage structure that would consistently keep wage levels well below 50% of the club's total income. In their efforts to catch up, other clubs would break this structure over and over again and Liverpool would be among them, continuing to outspend their far more successful rivals in the transfer market for the rest of the decade.

During his five games in charge against United, Souness would field a remarkable total of eighteen new players, collectively costing more than £16.5 million. In contrast, Fergie fielded only seven debutants during that time, at a cost of only a little more than half that amount, and almost half of that had gone on Keane. He, along with Giggs, Schmeichel, and Cantona would of course play an enormous role in United's success over the rest of the decade. In contrast, seven of those new players would cost Liverpool over a million each, but only two of them (Wright and Ruddock) would go on to feature in United-Liverpool games on more than two occasions.

These laughable claims were part of a continuing tendency for Liverpool supporters to define themselves in terms of their opposition to United. An increasing Anyone-But-United (ABU) culture was rising in the English game as is became clear the Reds were finally fulfilling their potential as the country's dominant club. Liverpool fans sought refuge within this network of envy and bitterness, seeing their own club as the rightful leaders of any campaign fuelled by such dubious values. In doing so, they sacrificed any true claims to greatness on behalf of a club who, until very recently, had occupied that position themselves.

All this really shows, of course, is how United were winning battles off the pitch as well as on them, bolstered by a sound (if admittedly depressingly over-commercialised) business approach and led by a manager who was happy to have money to spend when he needed it, but slept much more easily knowing he oversaw a solid wage structure, frugal spending in the transfer market and a youth development policy that was rapidly regaining its reputation as the best in the country.

Although emerging rivals like Arsenal would mount a more sustained challenge in the late nineties with a far more balanced approach to buying and spending, other clubs were mortgaging their futures simply in order to stay in the game. The likes of Aston Villa, Blackburn, Newcastle and

Leeds would all spend heavily in an attempt to get anywhere near to United, and all would be paying for their folly well into the future. Only Liverpool's merchandising power – second only to United among English clubs – would prevent them from falling away just as dramatically. Of course, many Liverpool fans would criticise United for soul-selling via capitalist trappings like sponsorship and shirt deals as if they were a feature of the modern game that the Reds alone had bought into. As usual, the facts were somewhat different. Liverpool had actually been the first English club to feature a sponsor's logo on their shirts, way back in 1979, three years before United desecrated their own shirts in a similar way. [5] The relationship between Liverpool FC and filthy lucre is just as close as that involving any other major club, and closer than most.

Liverpool's poor use of that money was evident not only in the frequent two million-plus deals in the transfer market that consistently failed to pay off, but in the quick turnaround of players initially celebrated as hidden gems by Koppites, only to be forgotten and brushed under the carpet as they moved on, often within a couple of years. At the end of this season players like Hutchison and Piechnik would have gone, while others like Paul Stewart and Mark Walters continued to hang on, only to have their similarly unfulfilled reputations as potential world-beaters brushed under the Anfield carpet when they eventually left.

By the time of this game, the vultures were circling around Souness. Given the failure of so many big signings to deliver, that was inevitable, although a successful United can't have helped him either. Indeed, there are many United fans who still regard the 1993-94 team as the best Ferguson ever put together. We'd been top of the league since 23 August and would stay there until the end of the season, only the nouveau riche of Blackburn Rovers getting close enough even to have us in their sights as the Reds shoved the views of those who'd written off the previous season as a one-off firmly down their throats.

Although they'd experienced disappointment with an early departure from the European Cup at the hands of Galatasary, domestically United were untouchable, playing with fluency and penetration with the flexibility of Cantona and Hughes up front, supported by any two out of any three of Giggs, Sharpe and Kanchelskis on the wing, with Keane and Ince providing a formidable spine in the midfield. Any occasional weaknesses in defence were shrugged off: United just scored more than our opponents, brilliantly exemplified earlier in the season when, inspired by a relentless Keane and unstoppable Cantona, the Reds had overturned a two-goal deficit at city to come back and win 3-2. At this point in the season, the only blemish on United's record was a single defeat at Chelsea. We were 21 points ahead of Liverpool.

All of which pointed, surely, to a convincing victory at Liverpool when the two clubs eventually met. And, early in the game, that's exactly how it looked. After 24 minutes, the Reds were already 3-0 up and showed no signs of resting on their laurels; with the internet still very much in its infancy, no United fan had the technology yet to Google the biggest margin of victory for a United team at Anfield, though older fans may well have recalled the 4-1 victory there in 1969. At that stage, beating that score looked a formality and those of greater years, or else furnished with the knowledge of more obscure facts, may well have suggested that matching or beating the 5-0 drubbing meted out in the War League of 1946 was now well within our sights. Bruce had opened the scoring in the ninth minute, getting his head to Irwin's inch perfect far post cross from the left. Giggs scored the second, seizing on Redknapp's misplaced pass to Wright before lobbing Grobbelaar brilliantly from outside the box. Ruddock's wild hack at Keane led to United's third, resulting in the free kick that Irwin dispatched into the top left corner.

At that point, it seemed only a matter of time before we added to our haul. However, a clearly wounded Liverpool recovered some pride to change the direction of the game within minutes of Irwin's strike, Clough's long range shot giving Schmeichel no chance. As the game moved towards half-time, Clough struck again, racing into the area to wrong-foot the United keeper with a clinical finish. Then, with United hell-bent on re-establishing a two goal margin before the break, Giggs somehow managed to send the ball backwards in the Liverpool area with the goal gaping before him

The youngster was then denied by a fine save from Grobbelaar (in what would prove to be his last Liverpool-United game) in the second half, before Schmeichel matched him to push away a shot from McManaman and his opposite number even applauded at the other end when the Dane flew to his left to keep out an effort from Dicks. It was a match played in that kind of spirit: indeed, it was a characteristic of Souness's reign at Liverpool that, for a brief spell at least, a certain civility between the playing staff of the two clubs, if not the supporters, was evident during these encounters. Souness had, of course, been Fergie's mystery ally in the notorious 'Get Rush' Scotland controversy of 1986 and it was clear a strong mutual respect prevailed between the two men.

The scoring in this cracking game was completed eleven minutes before time when Ruddock rose in the area with a bullet header that gave Schmeichel no chance. Although Liverpool fans celebrated a fine comeback, they were aware that this was but a minor hitch in United's onward march to the title. You sensed that, for them, it was more a sense of relief that they'd avoided the stuffing that had looked on the cards early in the game, as well as an opportunity to witness a welcome and all too rare display of pride among those wearing the club's shirt that had provoked their euphoria.

It wasn't enough to save Souness' job though. This impressive show of character proved to be his last game in charge against United as he resigned later in the month. In terms of league form, the timing was perhaps surprising: Liverpool had been unbeaten since the beginning of December and followed this result with a convincing win at Oldham and a home win against city. However, a humiliating defeat at Bristol City in the FA Cup brought about the meeting with the board and the calling of time on the former captain's less than glittering period in charge as manager. He would be the first Liverpool manager to be removed from the job since Don Welsh back in 1956.

With Liverpool supporters heavily in favour of re-establishing the link to the era of the Boot Room, the club appointed Roy Evans as his successor: gone would be the mutual respect of Souness' three year tenure as Evans at least proved himself a worthy protector of the Anfield club's persecution complex, if little else. He'd cement his popularity among the fans with statements beginning 'I wonder if anyone outside Merseyside remembers...' simultaneously recalling the club's past while fuelling the collective paranoia of a support convinced no one had ever given them the credit they deserved. The fact that is was now difficult to claim they even deserved any such credit was, for the moment, neatly brushed under the carpet as the fans anticipated a new golden age under Evans that, inevitably, never came.

Liverpool: Grobbelaar, Dicks, Wright, Jones, Ruddock, Redknapp, Clough, McManaman (Bjornabye), Barnes, Fowler, Rush.

United: Schmeichel, Parker, Pallister, Bruce, Irwin, Keane, Ince, Kanchelskis, McClair, Giggs, Cantona.

Attendance: 42,795

Performance record (Ferguson v Souness)

Games – 5
United wins – 1
Draws – 3
Liverpool wins – 1
United goals – 7
Liverpool goals - 6

Honours

Manchester United – 1 Premier League; 1 European Cup Winners' Cup; 1
League Cup; 1 FA Charity Shield; 1 European Super Cup
Liverpool – 1 FA Cup

Transfer expenditure

Incoming transfers
Manchester United – £8.58 million
Liverpool – £17.94 million

Outgoing transfers
Manchester United – £3.19 million
Liverpool – £9.83 million

Net spend
Manchester United – £5.39 million
Liverpool – £8.11 million

References

1. P Barclay, Football: Bloody Hell, pp259-260
2. **www.theguardian.com/football/2001/nov/17/sport.comment1**
3. P Auclair, Cantona, p239
4. ibid, p238
5. **www.theguardian.com/football/2002/sep/28/newsstory.sport**
6. P Auclair, Cantona, p216

3

Fear of a Red Planet

Ferguson v Evans

30 March 1994

Manchester United 1 Liverpool 0

It said much about the level of expectations among United fans these days that we approached this second meeting of the season in a mood of some disappointment. Until the previous weekend, the serious prospect of an unprecedented domestic treble had been on the cards. Unfortunately, the Reds had lost the League Cup Final to Aston Villa. It was a surprise defeat and, given that the league was in the bag and the other teams remaining in the FA Cup didn't appear to present any reason for serious concern (we'd again drawn Oldham in the semi-final), United fans would have been optimistic of bagging all three trophies if we'd been successful at Wembley.

Such disappointment was, of course, also a reflection on the elevated mood around Old Trafford. Those of us who'd lived through the meagre Sexton years, the false dawns of Atkinson and the grim reality checks of the early Ferguson period had to admit that it was a very welcome turnaround to support a club still, with less than two months of the season to go, on course for our first league and cup double. Set against what we'd endured for years, we could probably put up with the occasional setback in the League Cup. Indeed, with designs in the future soon to be more firmly set on the still elusive prospect of success in Europe, the defeat to Villa would mark the point where Ferguson and United ceased to give serious attention to the competition.

This positive mood had been subdued when the news came through, shortly after the previous Liverpool game, that the great Matt Busby had passed away. Understandably, a mood of grief prevailed around Old Trafford even as the Reds continued their surge towards yet more silverware. A sickening barometer of the contempt in which United were held across much of English football came in the minute's silence for a man who stood as one of very few in the English game to have established a great club and in the process changed English football. It is to the credit of Liverpool fans that the bulk of their support upheld the silence that took place across football grounds the weekend after his passing: a reminder that, particularly in the wake of what happened at Hillsborough, there was now at least some sense of mutual respect between the two clubs in the aftermath of tragedy and sadness. Unfortunately, many other rival fans failed to follow their lead, most notably those of Leeds, whose own players vociferously made their objections known to the chants from the away end that rang out throughout the silence prior to their game at Blackburn. As well as revealing much about the distasteful character of a significant element among the Leeds support, it was another reminder of the deep levels of hatred that persisted in relation to United across the country. Former Liverpool boss Dalglish, now manager at Blackburn, deserved credit for being among those to come out and strongly condemn the behaviour.

In the league, only another defeat to Chelsea (this time at home) had interrupted a smooth run towards the title. And there was every sign that, despite the comeback they'd mounted in January, this Liverpool side didn't possess anything that might throw us even slightly off track. As expected, the arrival of Roy Evans had offered the comfort of past memories to fans more than happy to wrap themselves in nostalgia, while doing little to remove the crushing oppression of the present. Permanently on the defensive these days, their fans resorted instead to ABU baiting and desperate claims that United's football was, as one Liverpool fan put it to me, simple 'a pale reflection of the old Liverpool style'. They got heavily behind the nouveau riche of Blackburn, apparently believing that now they were managed by Dalglish their high league placing had somehow something to do with them Thus, a convincing defeat at Blackburn the previous month could be borne with equanimity fortified by the faint hope that Dalglish's new team might still catch United. In reality, this hope was as futile as their own prospects of challenging for anything meaningful any time soon.

Here, we picked them off without breaking sweat, Paul Ince's near-post header from a corner enough to secure a routine victory en route to retaining our championship. There would be hiccups to come – we lost at both Blackburn, briefly reviving their hopes, and Wimbledon in April – but went on to win the league by eight points. We were close to blowing the FA Cup, though. Only Mark Hughes's stunning equaliser a minute from the end of extra time prevented Oldham from getting a rare tilt at glory, although we quickly put that behind us to win the replay 4-1. We faced Chelsea in the final – a club who'd achieved an unlikely double over us that season – but put on a relentless display of attacking football to which the Londoners had no answer. Although it took an hour for us to open the scoring through Cantona, we went on to win 4-0, ABUs everywhere subsequently inundating radio phone-ins with anguished calls that the second goal should never have been a penalty. It's true it was a close call but hardly detracted from United's dominance in the second half. The calls, it seemed, simply reflected the desperation of United haters, for whom desperation was now a way of life.

United: Schmeichel, Parker, Bruce, Pallister, Irwin, Sharpe (Giggs), Keane, Kanchelskis, Ince, Hughes, Cantona (Robson).

Liverpool: James, Jones, Nicol, Dicks, Ruddock, Whelan, Thomas (Fowler), McManaman, Redknapp, Barnes, Rush.

Attendance: 44,751

17 September 1994

Manchester United 2 Liverpool 0

United's ultimate failure to defend that double successfully has generally been put down to the loss of Cantona later in the campaign (more of which later) and there's no question that this played a part. However, there were already signs early in the campaign that the triumphant side of the last two years might need freshening up sooner rather than later. The only signing the Reds had made the previous summer had been the capture of David May from Blackburn Rovers, clearly a signing for the future rather than anything likely to spruce up a team in danger of resting on its laurels.

Perhaps it was simply the case that Ferguson felt there was no such danger: the side, after all, was packed with leaders and that was one of its most significant strengths. The likes of Bruce, Ince, Keane and Cantona gave you captains all over the pitch: there was no need to fire them up with additional competition for places, surely? The early signs suggested something different. Although we won this game at a canter, the victory was sandwiched between defeats at Leeds and Ipswich before another reverse at Sheffield Wednesday made it three away reverses on the trot.

By that point United would be struggling in fifth place and, with Blackburn Rovers with money to spend and looking determined to build significantly on their progress of the previous season, there were clearly more significant obstacles for the Reds to negotiate this time if they were to repeat either of the successes of the previous season. A newly introduced group stage in the Champions League meant greater fixture congestion in the early part of the season: for that reason, United would put out essentially a team of reserves – a very promising team of reserves, admittedly – and go down to defeat at Newcastle in the League Cup. It evidently didn't help much: another Champions League campaign came to nothing when the Reds fell to defeats at Barcelona and, crucially, IFK Goteborg to miss out on qualification from the group stage.

You wonder, viewing these early setbacks and the many positive signs evident among the youngsters who acquitted themselves so well at Newcastle in the League Cup, whether Ferguson's mind was already pondering the upheavals of the following summer, where he would surprise pretty much everybody by breaking up his first successful team without, on the face of it, replacing the key players who would be on their way. There were already signs: youngsters Nicky Butt and Gary Neville would feature in a number of league games that season, the latter beginning to establish himself at right back in place of the injured Paul Parker. Indeed, aside from the already established Giggs, thirteen recent products of the youth team would feature in the first team at some point during season. Andy Cole would arrive from Newcastle in January, signalling a break-up of the Cantona-Hughes partnership and paving the way for Sparky's eventual departure. There was, in other words, more transition afoot during the season than many people appeared to realise at the time, meaning that perhaps United fans ought not to have been quite so surprised at the events to come in summer 1995.

One thing that didn't change was superiority over Liverpool, which was evident again in this game. Here, our rivals certainly contributed to their own downfall, a pitiful attempt at a headed back pass from John Scales letting in Kanchelskis to score the opener. Liverpool were stlll reeling from that when a slick passing move involving Cantona and McClair led to the Scotsman's clinical finish and three points for United.

Liverpool fans predictably wailed about the fortunate nature of the opening goal, as if we simply weren't allowed to exploit their many glaring weaknesses, let alone one from a defender that had cost them three million quid. They would go on to win the League Cup that season, allowing Evans – as Souness had with his FA Cup triumph – to hint at a promise that was never really there. The trophy did leave a number of United fans a tad disappointed that we'd allowed them an easy route to silverware by not taking the competition seriously ourselves that year.

Otherwise, it was gratifyingly business as usual for the Anfield side. In addition to spending £3.5 million to buy in Scales from Wimbledon, Phil Babb was recruited as a central defensive partner for only slightly less a day later. Laughable as Liverpool fans' claims were that it wasn't 'the Liverpool way' to indulge in lavish spending, it was perhaps understandable when so many of these expensive signings then proceeded to look like no more than mediocre journeymen.

They had, admittedly, begun the league campaign with three victories, scoring freely, but a home draw with West Ham followed by this defeat showed their true, still fading colours. Nonetheless, the combination of those early victories along with the amount of money the club were clearly prepared to spend was leading to an outbreak of optimism at Anfield that offered an ironic perspective on their current situation: supporters who had once witnessed genuinely dominant teams on a frequent basis were now proclaiming glorious new dawns on the most flimsy, or simply non-existent, evidence.

United: Schmeichel, Bruce, May, Pallister, Irwin, Ince, Giggs, Sharpe, Kanchelskis, Hughes (McClair), Cantona.

Liverpool: James, Jones, Bjornabye, Ruddock, Scales, Molby (Babb), McManaman, Redknapp, Barnes, Rush, Fowler.

Attendance: 43,470

19 March 1995

Liverpool 2 Manchester United 0

Conventional wisdom has it that United's season fell apart on 25 January when Eric Cantona, with actions described in the media with words usually reserved for serial killers or third world dictators, had responded to his red card by wildly kicking out at a Crystal Palace supporter who'd come down to the front to bait him. There was no doubt it was a violent attack, nor that it was clearly going to lead to a lengthy ban, although, speaking as somebody who had witnessed two such altercations in non-league games and still recalled Birmingham's Alberto Tarantina wading into the stands to attack supporters without any ban ensuing, the coverage seemed a tad sensationalised.

It was, of course, the United factor that made it so, coupled with a view that had never gone away that, beneath his talented exterior, Cantona was a troublemaker that many simply wanted out of English football. I say nothing to justify the attack although, on a human level, I've always felt that the idea football players had to show restraint when on the receiving end of the most extreme abuse a ridiculous notion. I say this having, in the eighties, witnessed fans making monkey noises at black players while stewards laughed along with them, as well as the outrage shown by fans at those two non-league games when the individuals on the pitch responded in an perfectly understandable way to the cowards in the crowd, who assumed a wall between them and the receivers of their vile abuse allowed them to behave as obnoxiously as they wished.

Anyway, the result was we were without Cantona for the rest of the season and for the early months of the following campaign. It's often made me laugh when defenders of future offenders who'd receive six game bans or some such insubstantial punishment would howl, 'But it's no worse than what Cantona did,' conveniently forgetting, or simply ignoring, that he received an eight month ban. Admittedly, there were games in which we would miss him: he'd been magnificent prior to the ban as United put their early season setbacks behind them, losing only one of seventeen league games up to the Selhurst Park incident and moving onto the shoulder of leaders Blackburn.

However, apart from a defeat at Everton in February, that form had continued despite the loss of Cantona, United having moved briefly to the top of the league the week before that game before returning to the top, again briefly, in early March. Without him we racked up the biggest ever win in the Premier League, a 9-0 defeat of Ipswich, Andy Cole putting his early detractors in their place by bagging five goals, and would lose only one further game in the league that season, although it was inevitably particularly disappointing that it had to be this one.

Even worse, the defeat would prove decisive in terms of United's chances of again retaining our title. On a rain-soaked Sunday afternoon Liverpool took the game to us and got their reward in the first half when Redknapp finished off a passing move with help from some inept United defending. The Reds contributed heavily to the second goal too, Bruce deflecting McManaman's seemingly harmless shot past his own keeper. The defeat left United six points adrift of Blackburn at the top.

Had the Reds simply fallen away in the race for the league at that point, it might have been less painful in the long run. But, whatever plans Fergie had for the summer, this was still a United side that didn't know when to give up and they fought their way back into the title race as Blackburn faltered towards the finishing line. The rest is Premier League history. On the final day of the campaign, United needed to win at West Ham while hoping that Blackburn lost at, of all places, Anfield. Understandably, there were expectations that, in welcoming the returning Dalglish, a Liverpool side with nothing to play for would simply lie down and allow Blackburn's stumbling progress to the championship to reach its conclusion. In the event, what happened was far worse.

It was no surprise that the Kop was full of Blackburn scarves. I'll admit that there have been many occasions in the past when I wanted Liverpool to lose a vital game and that, had the situations been reversed, it would have been hard to want to see my own side hand them victory on a plate. However, I can't imagine ever wearing the colours of another club and I know many onlookers who watched on television, shaking their heads at how low many Liverpool fans could stoop when it came to anything involving United.

To their credit, their players weren't buying into that and, to pretty much everyone's surprise, including many of their own supporters, they did the honourable thing and went on to beat Blackburn 2-1. Meanwhile, in London, United had come from behind to draw level at West Ham via a Brian McClair goal early in the second half. With the remainder of the game pretty much spent in front of the home side's goal, it was surely only a matter of time before United scored. Except we didn't. To the delight of everyone at Anfield, news filtered through that United had failed to get that second goal and they had the double delight of celebrating victory for their team as well as the league championship for Blackburn.

And it got worse. Liverpool fans exchanged their Blackburn scarves, shamefully, for those of their local rivals as a clearly out of sorts United then fell to Everton in the FA Cup Final. It was horrible. The devastated feelings of 1992 returned in only slightly different form and the haters decided that United's successful period had after all been a temporary glitch and we'd now revert to our pre-1993 ways. Although few will admit it now, when the events of the summer began to unfurl, some United fans began to agree with them.

Liverpool: James, Wright, Bjornabye, Ruddock, Babb, Scales, McManaman, Redknapp, Barnes (Thomas), Fowler, Rush (Walters).

United: Schmeichel, Pallister, Bruce, Irwin, Sharpe (Cole), Kanchelskis, Ince, Giggs, Keane (Butt), McClair, Hughes.

Attendance: 38,906

1 October 1995

Manchester United 2 Liverpool 2

Former Liverpool captain Alan Hansen's 'You'll win nothing with kids' remark would haunt him throughout the rest of his media career. They were made during the first Match of the Day of the season after a new look United side had succumbed meekly to defeat at Aston Villa. It's now the stuff of legend that United would shove his words firmly back down his throat, though it's less well documented how many United fans of the time were saying something similar.

They'd watched on in horror as the gruesome end to the 1994-95 season was followed by the departure of Paul Ince to Inter Milan, Mark Hughes to Chelsea and Andrei Kanchelskis, who'd been the previous season's top scorer in league games, to Everton. No new signings had come in to replace them. Even worse, there were persistent rumours throughout the summer that Cantona, despondent over his constant haranguing by the British media, was also set to leave. It seemed the best United side for almost three decades was falling apart and many assumed that Ferguson, following the disappointments of the previous season, had simply lost it. A Manchester Evening News poll during the summer revealed that the majority of respondents thought the United manager should go (though it was probably partly sabotaged by city fans).

Of course, history has proved Ferguson not only correct but brilliant in his management of the situation. Like any truly great manager, he hadn't been afraid to court public discontentment when he was certain he was doing the right thing. Later it would emerge that Ince, nicknamed the 'guv'nor' among his colleagues, had become too big a challenge to the manager's dressing room authority. Kanchelskis had been transfer listed following demands that he play more regularly, a bargain the manager wasn't willing to strike. Hughes had simply got to the age where letting him go for £1.5 million represented good value, especially following the signing of Andy Cole.

The manager knew, of course, that he already had players within the club to replace them. Players like David Beckham and Paul Scholes would go on to become club legends; they had already made their debuts for United and were among a group of youngsters who'd established a tremendous reputation at youth level. Gary Neville and Nicky Butt were already regular members of the first team squad and Gary's brother Phil was also on the verge of regular action. All five youngsters featured in this game, all, with the exception of Butt, making their first appearance in a United-Liverpool game. It was still a subject of much debate whether these players could really step into the shoes of the legendary figure on their way out of the club, but Ferguson had the courage of his convictions and knew he had to give them first team opportunities in order to secure their futures at the club. What better statement of belief could you show talented youngsters that to allow three senior players to leave and not sign any replacements? So Fergie went ahead and, with criticisms from friend and foe alike ringing in his ears, made the single most important and far-reaching decision in United's recent history.

While happy to allow some senior players to leave, he knew he had to do everything possible to keep Cantona at the club. It's testimony to the important role of the Frenchman and Ferguson's appreciation of it that he was never tempted to do what he was advised from so many quarters and cut his losses on a player who, next time his indiscretions got the better of him, might well get an even longer ban or, worse, follow his exile from French football with a similar fate in England. Fergie took those risks on the chin, pleaded with him to stay at the club and got his rewards, both on and off the pitch. Cantona, in spite of his reputation outside Old Trafford, was a model professional and would become a vital nurturing figure for the young players coming through. He would also, Fergie knew, respond to his show of faith in him in exactly the right way.

For United fans Cantona was already far more than just a talented player who'd been the single most important factor in bringing about the successes of recent years. He was a figure who represented the soul of the club, a talisman with a significance that already saw him lining up alongside figures like George Best as among the most important ever to wear the red shirt of United. That wasn't in spite of his wayward reputation, but partly because of it. He exemplified the spirit and character of his club in a manner that other clubs, and particularly Liverpool, could never understand.

As would be emphasised with the Suarez affair (of which more later), Liverpool fans really didn't know how to respond to a player of unquestioned talent whose character might be somewhat flawed. While I'm sure there are United fans shallow enough to have claimed Cantona's character to be a completely unblemished one, I believe the majority view among Reds was to recognise that our hero had a dark side but to regard that as no reason to stop loving him; indeed, to love him not merely in spite of it but partly because of it. That red devil on the badge is not there for nothing: it means something and we love players who represent the outsider spirit that's part of United's DNA and, still more, do it with some style. From the point of view of Cantona, you wonder how much he knew of this when he joined the club and how much of it was running through his head on that day in November 1992 when he stood beside Alex Ferguson surveying his new surroundings for the first time before deciding this was the place for him to see out the rest of his career.

When the fixtures for the new season were announced, it was revealed that, when Cantona's ban ended at the end of September, his first game would be against Liverpool at Old Trafford. The game also came at a time when we were badly in need of him. Newcastle had stormed to an early lead in the Premiership with a brand of attacking football that was winning them friends all across the country, particularly in households desperate for someone other than United to take over at the top, Blackburn's laughable efforts in Europe – which had made

United's own pitiful attempts look something like a genuine tilt at glory – meant few now saw them as a meaningful long-term proposition. Admittedly, United once again hardly covered themselves in European glory, exiting the UEFA Cup in the first round following defeat on away goals to Rotor Volograd, against whom Schmeichel had come up to grab a late equaliser for the Reds that sadly still wasn't enough.

United were still in contention for the league, however, with that defeat at Aston Villa proving nothing like as ominous as Hansen had predicted. After it had come five successive league wins and, although many had scoffed at a 3-0 reverse to York City in the League Cup, this was because few yet understood the low priority United were beginning to give the competition. And because, of course, they were desperate for signs that we were no longer a threat. It turned out to be our only home defeat of the season.

Newcastle admittedly looked the real deal though, and it was clear United would need to fire on all cylinders to have a decent chance of reclaiming the league championship. In truth, our performance against Liverpool, despite the enormous significance of Cantona's return to action, suggested any such challenge was still some way off. United did open the scoring within only two minutes and, typically, Cantona had a hand in the goal, his cross from the left finding Nicky Butt storming into the area to finish and get the Reds off to the best possible start.

Liverpool's equaliser came through a storming effort from Fowler, thrashing the ball home from the left of the penalty area, and the same player gave the visitors the lead in the second half, again arriving from the left to outmuscle Gary Neville and lob Schmeichel. United's equaliser, when it came, was all the more satisfying for the way Liverpool fans would still be moaning about it months later. Cantona brought the ball forward from midfield and played an excellent weighted pass into the path of Giggs who, according to the referee, was tumbled to the ground by Redknapp and, according to Liverpool supporters, threw himself to the turf with a contempt for human decency that lay somewhere between Charlie Manson and Fred West. The fact that Redknapp walked meekly away rather than protest the decision suggested he knew referee David Ellary had got it right but Liverpool fans were never going to let facts like that come between them and an outbreak of righteous outrage.

Inevitably, Cantona stepped up to take the penalty and, just as inevitably, scored. He almost set up a winner too, his floated ball into the box finding Andy Cole, only for his strike partner's flamboyant scissor-kick to drop wide of the goal.

The attendance figure below again requires some explanation. Ahead of the European Championships the following summer, ground redevelopment was taking place that would eventually take Old Trafford's capacity above 55,000. These plans for expansion were actually being drawn long before Fergie won his first trophy, United clearly having faith perhaps not so much that they were on the road to eventual success but that United's remarkable support would still be around in large numbers no matter what the future held. Indeed, even though this work would limit attendance figures at the ground until late March, the Reds would still have the best average attendance of any English club over the season.

United: Schmeichel, G Neville, P Neville (Scholes), Bruce, Pallister, Sharpe, Butt (Beckham), Keane, Cole, Cantona, Giggs.

Liverpool: James, McAteer, Babb, Rush, Scales, Redknapp, Thomas, McManaman. Harkness, Fowler, Ruddock.

Attendance: 34,934

17 December 1995

Liverpool 2 Manchester United 0

Although United remained second in the league after this defeat, the gap with leaders Newcastle widened and would continue to do so as the Reds followed this setback with defeat at Leeds and a crushing 4-1 reverse at Spurs on New Years Day. Crucially, a win against Newcastle on Boxing Day prevented it from becoming a chasm, but even so the Reds would be ten points adrift going into the New Year. Across the country, fans were in 'give it to them now' mood and, inevitably, this included Liverpool supporters, who saw this result as confirmation that United wouldn't be regaining the Premier League trophy any time soon. In the spirit of the time, many were now happy to shelve the 'traitor' accusations levelled against Keegan when he left them for Hamburg in order to reclaim him as another Anfield old boy about to put one over on United.

That it wouldn't turn out that way is down, in roughly equal proportions, to United's character set against Newcastle's lack of it. Much has been made of Keegan's end of season explosion on Sky Sports when his side had all but handed the trophy to a United who had simply not done what everyone else wanted them to and given in. Keegan's animated and incoherent display was taken as a sign that he'd 'lost it': however, the process that led to Newcastle surrendering the trophy had begun long before that. Many understandably pointed to the ill-fated signing of Colombian Faustino Asprilla and Keegan's obsessive attempts to shoehorn him into a side that had been doing perfectly well without him. It wasn't so much Asprilla himself that was the problem: he was clearly a talented player, albeit one who needed time to adapt to the game in this country. Rather it was a lack of that crucial managerial touch that knows when to exercise change and when to leave well alone, when to add something to the mix and when to know you were in danger of leaving the pudding seriously over-egged. Ferguson had it and Keegan didn't. And that, more than anything, was what determined the fate of the Premier League that season.

The case of Asprilla emphasised something else about Keegan, too. He constantly referred to him by his nickname 'Tino' in interviews. It would be a forerunner of Steve McLaren's cringing references to 'Stevie G' in his brief and unsuccessful stint as manager of England. The tendency revealed both to be essentially fans of the game thrust into management situations that were too big for them. That was what made them likeable for many people: but, ultimately, would they be prepared to risk that popularity in order to take that vital step towards success? It was the one ingredient that set Fergie aside from his managerial rivals and, until Wenger and later Mourinho came along, he would find himself without peers in this area in English football management. My guess is that neither Wenger nor Mourinho, nor the teams they managed, would have buckled in the way Keegan and Newcastle did.

It meant that Fergie, rather than responding with desperation to defeats like this one, had a formula he believed was a winning one and stuck to his guns. It was precisely the same mentality that, in the summer, had encouraged him to fly in the face of just about all opinion and stick to his faith in this combination of young charges and tried and tested winners.

For this match, United were wearing their much-derided grey kits: these would become infamous when, at half-time during a defeat at

Southampton (their only time the team would lose that season after the loss at Spurs) they changed into different shirts, Ferguson explaining that his players couldn't see each other in the grey ones. The United manager was roundly scoffed at for what was seen as a pitiful excuse. However, it was another example of his managerial expertise: whether or not the shirts really had any significance (and United were wearing them on four of the five occasions they suffered defeat in the league that season) wasn't really the point: psychologically, if it helped his players deal with a setback that might otherwise derail their late tilt at the league title, that was all that mattered. It was, in its small way, yet another example of how Fergie stood well above any of his managerial rivals in terms of psychology and an his understanding of the details that went into the production of a winning mentality.

For now, however, there were no exchanges at half-time and no fingers pointed at the grey shirts. United simply continued to look unconvincing title challengers and Liverpool took full advantage: although the home side went into the game with a poor run behind them of only one win in six games, they appeared to have little difficulty in overpowering their rivals here. Once again it was Fowler who did the damage, opening the scoring with a free kick just before half-time and sealing the win when he latched onto a McManaman pass to grab another in the closing minutes. In truth, it could have been more, with only the agility of Schmeichel keeping United from a truly embarrassing scoreline.

Ferguson understandably showed his disappointment at both performance and result in the press conference afterwards, excusing his younger players of blame - it was, after all, the first game at Anfield for most of them - and pointing the finger, Schmeichel excepted, at senior members of his team. 'That was the most lifeless performance I've seen from us,' he fumed.[1] Although there would be other lifeless performances to come, most notably at Spurs fifteen days later, the turning point wouldn't be far off, although even hardened optimists among the United support were struggling to find signs of it at the time.

Liverpool: James, Jones, McAteer, Wright, Collymore, Barnes, Scales, Thomas, McManaman, Harkness, Fowler.

United: Schmeichel, G Neville, Irwin, Bruce, May, Sharpe, McClair, Beckham, Cole (Scholes), Cantona, Giggs.

Attendance: 40,546

11 May 1996

FA Cup Final

Wembley

Manchester United 1 Liverpool 0

Who could have imagined, when the two sides last met, that the season would end up like this? Aside from the notorious 'grey shirts' match at Southampton, United had been unbeaten in all competitions after New Year's Day and a season that began with serious doubts about Ferguson's judgement ended with his team overcoming what had once looked an unbridgeable gap behind Newcastle by securing the league with victory over Middlesbrough on the last day of the league season. Aside from the three goals shipped at Southampton, the Reds had only conceded five goals in sixteen league games while, in a vital run of games in March, ten points from an available twelve had been secured with a single goal from Cantona in each of the four matches. Vitally, that had included a 1-0 win at Newcastle, where Schmeichel had produced a series of outstanding saves to keep the home side at bay before Cantona grabbed a crucial winner early in the second half.

It was just as nail-biting in the FA Cup. Andy Cole popped up with a third round replay winner at Sunderland to prevent the agony of a penalty shoot out. Manchester city fans had been incensed in the fifth round when United had been awarded a joke of a penalty that nobody in the ground had even appealed for before going on to win the game. City's season had continued to fall away after that point and, to the added glee of United fans, they were relegated on the same day the Reds celebrated winning the league. Their defeat against Liverpool that day was one of the very rare occasions when Reds fans were delighted with a win for the Anfield club.

Victory by the odd goal over Chelsea in the semi-finals had set up this, a final encounter with Liverpool for the first time since that famous treble-denying victory in 1977. United stood poised to become the first side in English history to secure a second double. Liverpool, having been denied that honour on several occasions, would surely be fully focused on ensuring it didn't happen.

One glance out onto the pitch at Wembley before the game, however, put any such thoughts to bed.

Clinical, unflashy efficiency had been Liverpool's watchword in their glory days. We'd assumed that the prospect of an increasingly rare tilt at at trophy, while at the same time ensuring United's season finished on a negative note, would be enough to focus them, at least temporarily, in that devastatingly successful manner of old.

So what the hell were they doing out on the Wembley pitch, pissing around in white suits?

If anything brought even more optimism to the already buoyant United support it was this. Liverpool FC, of all teams, were out on the Wembley pitch, laughing and joking in flamboyant attire, acting as if they were taking part in some kind of Celebrity It's A Knockout rather than the final of the FA Cup against their biggest rivals. Meanwhile, in the pubs of Liverpool, local resentment was fuelled by thousands of Everton fans across the city turning up decked out in the grey United kits that were now being sold off cheap by sports shops, eager to see their city rivals defeated. Liverpool supporters had, of course, got fully behind Everton in their final against United the previous year, but now Evertonians showed the 'all in it together' Merseyside spirit to be the Anfield-concocted farce we'd always known it was.

Instead, Everton fans joined the rest of the world in mocking these fancy suits, a symbol that the Liverpool FC of old truly were dead, replaced by these imposters, the self-styled 'Spice Boys', many of whom were, it was widely suspected, putting modelling contracts before success on the pitch. Finally, the penny dropped as to why, in their great days, Liverpool had only signed ugly players. What, after all, were the chances of players who earned a good chunk of their income from modeling contracts going in where it hurts? We pointed at the white suits and laughed, while giving thanks for Steve Bruce.

Incidentally, Bruce was missing from the starting line up in this game, following an unbroken run of nineteen starts in United-Liverpool contests, a record for consecutive appearances in the fixture that would never be beaten during the Ferguson era. Brucey would leave the club in the summer, opting for first team football at Birmingham City having been told his time as an automatic first choice for United was coming to an end. He would, needless to say, remain a club legend: one of the first and most crucial components of this great United side. Appearing as a substitute for Liverpool was Ian Rush, also in his final game, the last remaining player on either side from Fergie's first game between the clubs.

In the event, United laboured to defeat the Spice Boys. It was a deeply forgettable match. With both sides perhaps inhibited by a fear of losing, a dour midfield encounter of few chances and even fewer thrills ensued. For much of the game, this was frustrating viewing for Reds fans. Liverpool were clearly there for the taking and, long after their white suits had been discarded, they'd ceded control of the middle of the park to Roy Keane. Why, then, could United not take advantage?

Step up, once again, a certain E. Cantona. Fergie revealed years later that Cantona's influence on United's victory went beyond his performance on the field. Fergie had involved his senior players in tactical discussions prior to the game and it was Cantona's suggestion that Keane be deployed in a deep marking role to nullify the threat of McManaman that had stifled what United felt was Liverpool's one creative outlet. [2] Although the tactic did little to raise the entertainment level of the game, it worked like a treat in ensuring that United walked off with the trophy and another double.

Cantona's influence in the game itself has been more widely noted. When the ball fell to him four minutes from time, it seemed there was nothing on other than an opportunity to put a speculative ball into the box on what had been an afternoon littered with speculative balls into the box. As I watched, the memory of a friend's comment following United's late draw with QPR in March lodged in my mind at the very moment he shaped to take a shot. Cantona had scored the equaliser in stoppage time in that game and this friend, who wasn't even a football fan, had observed while watching the highlights with me that it had seemed that Cantona had always known he was going to score an equaliser, but had deliberately waited until the point at which the goal was most devastating for the opposition. I'd replied that, if that was the case, I wished he'd done it earlier to give us the chance of getting the winner but, as the ball appeared to take an age to leave Cantona's foot and somehow thread its way through the many bodies in the penalty area, I recalled his words.

The timing and precision of Cantona's shot were masterful: it was almost as if Aristole, applying both his physics and moral theory to football, had laid out the plan beforehand, leaving Cantona, armed with the supreme mechanism of the Golden Mean, to follow it at precisely the point when all of those bodies were lined up for maximum impact. I'm sorry if that sounds like pseudo bollocks, but it's Cantona we're talking about, after all. Anyway, it went in. The United end of the ground erupted. United's soul had been embodied in a perfect shot at the right time, in the right place and against the right opponents. This was as near as it got to footballing perfection and, had Aristotle been around to see it, he'd surely have agreed.

United: Schmeichel, May, Pallister, Irwin, P Neville, Beckham (G Neville), Giggs, Keane, Butt, Cole (Scholes), Cantona.

Liverpool: James, Wright, Jones (Thomas), Babb, Scales, McAteer, Redknapp, McManaman, Barnes, Fowler, Collymore (Rush).

Attendance: 79,007

12 October 1996

Manchester United 1 Liverpool 0

Following the completion of a second double, any lingering beliefs among rivals that the Reds' successful era had ended with the departure of Ince, Kanchelskis and Hughes had been completely demolished. Although Newcastle had beaten United to the signing of Alan Shearer from Blackburn they, like Shearer's previous club, turned out to be no more than big spending interlopers, unable to compete long-term with Ferguson's project. The glorious products of his youth team ought to have killed off there and then the allegation that United merely owed their success to deep pockets, but of course it didn't. Those who saw United's glorious run of honours as a nightmare they'd been for years denying could ever come true inevitably sought reasons to dismiss or devalue our achievements. The enormous spending of Blackburn, Newcastle and Liverpool was either overlooked, or simply justified in an attempt to overhaul a side that had even more money that they did. In truth, the nearest any of them had got to understanding the true scale of the problem before them was when Keegan had commented, following his side's defeat of Ferguson's youngsters in that 1994 League Cup game, that the quality of the young players coming through at United was the one thing his club couldn't match.

This was the real source of United's strength in the Ferguson era.

Between Russell Beardsmore and Lee Martin making their first appearances against Liverpool on New Year's Day 1989 and now, a total of 28 United players had made their bow in the fixture and a remarkable 11 of those were youth products. In the same time period only three – Marsh, McManaman and Fowler – had emerged from the youth set up at Anfield until Dominic Matteo featured in this game.

In the same period, those players introduced by United had collectively cost a little over £27 million, while Liverpool's exceeded £30 million. Yet this is only part of the story: more remarkably, during the period of Evans' tenure at Anfield, United actually brought in more from selling players than we'd spent in our transfer dealings. Much of this had come from the huge profits from the release of players like Ince and Kanchelskis, but the less publicised sale of the likes of Lee Martin and Mark Robins indicated another key benefit of the investment in youth: those who didn't make it at the club would move elsewhere, their value in the market bolstered by the reputation of United's youth strategy.

Throughout Fergie's time at United, more than fifty youth graduates would move on at a significant profit to the club (of course, many more would make a career in the game after being released for nothing). Transfer records for Liverpool show that, during the same period, the number of players who left their youth set up for a profit was well short of half that number. [3] It would be a mistake simply to point the finger at Liverpool for that, however, because it was very much part of the culture of the English game, and still is. A typical, and very revealing, quotation from the time, came from Karren Brady, then managing director at Birmingham City, who scrapped the club's youth scheme with the words 'baked bean companies don't grown their own beans'. [4]

None of this is to undervalue the enormous advantage that United's greater wealth gave them, of course (a wealth that, let us not forget either, was built on generations of vast support through thick and thin as well as the considerable foresight that went into the building of Old Trafford in the early years of the twentieth century). However, the Reds' success in the nineties was based far more on shrewd management of the youth system than is often appreciated even by our own supporters. In their attempts to match that success, other clubs like Liverpool opted for the kind of profligacy and over-spending that so many accused United of, in the process overlooking the facts and thus entirely missing the point. By the end of Roy Evans' time as manager, the Anfield club would have spent over £40 million on transfer fees, recovering barely a third of that amount through outgoing transfers, with only a single League Cup triumph to show for it.

United were reaping the benefits of the board's faith in Alex Ferguson in the late eighties and his shrewd investments in the youth set up and scouting network that had allowed the club, throughout the nineties, to concentrate significant spending on the occasional big name player judged by Ferguson to possess the kind of character that would thrive at United. It didn't always work out, of course. That summer Karel Poborsky, who'd shone for Czech Republic in Euro 96, was brought to Old Trafford, many assumed to take up the position on the right side of midfield vacated by Andrei Kanchelskis, Lee Sharpe having failed, despite his early potential, to make the position his own.

However, Poborsky would fail to reproduce his Czech Republic form any more than sporadically in a United shirt. Instead, David Beckham, finding the midfield positions difficult to break into due to the presence of Keane, Butt and now Paul Scholes, did what he would do so well throughout the rest of his career: he saw an opportunity and went for it. Displaying exactly the kind of character required by United and their manager, he did exactly what his good friend Gary Neville had done. Sensing a lack of opportunities in central defence, Neville had transformed himself into a right back and quickly established himself as first choice in the position. Beckham would do the same thing ahead of him on that right flank, putting in performances of consistent quality and in the process quickly becoming the best right-sided crosser of the ball in English football and perhaps anywhere else. Before long he'd seen off the challenge of Poborsky, who would make only fifteen starts in the league that season, a rare case of Alex Ferguson spending money that, as it turned out, hadn't needed to be spent.

Jordi Cruyff would prove similarly superfluous an addition to the United squad. Instead, the more low key signings of that close season proved to have far greater impact as United returned to European action with a determination to put in more of a challenge this time. Central defender Ronnie Johnsen proved a shrewd signing, albeit one whose long term impact would be restricted by injury, but it was his relatively unknown Norwegian compatriot Ole Gunnar Solskjaer who would turn out to be the most inspired addition to the playing staff. Solksjaer would exceed expectations by scoring 18 league goals in just 25 starts. Although many speculated that the arrival of Shearer might well have made United unstoppable on all fronts, it was clear from an early stage that this a lethal finisher with the face of a ten year old choir boy had what it took to thrive at Ferguson's United. Ultimately, Shearer had turned down United for a second time out of a desire to be a big fish in a small pond: given his talent, it would be rash to say he wouldn't have thrived at United, but that wasn't the kind of attitude, you sense, that would have warmed him to Ferguson. Instead, Solskjaer, a snip at £1.5 million, fitted the bill perfectly. He and Johnsen had cost United a combined total of less than three million, far less than Liverpool had spent on John Scales alone.

United's cruised to a single goal victory here without being at anything like our best. Unbeaten in the league at this point, the Reds secured the win thanks to a single goal from David Beckham. Beckham had announced himself to English football in the new season in the most spectacular way, scoring a sensational goal from his own half at Wimbledon in the opening game. Here, Solskjaer was dispossessed on the edge of the box, the loose ball falling to Beckham. whose shot, with what was quickly becoming the most celebrated right foot in English football, went in off the post.

Liverpool had a pretty good go at getting back into the game in the second half, but found an in-form Schmeichel in the way. The manner of the win suggested United were able to negotiate even high profile opponents in the Premier League in third gear. If the players believed that themselves, the run of games that followed would quickly make them think again. First, we were walloped 5-0 at Newcastle, the game memorable not just for the home side's rampant display but for a Geordie fatso running onto the pitch to prostrate himself before Keegan with 'we're not worthy' gestures. United then suffered a humiliating 6-3 defeat at Southampton before losing 2-1 at home to Chelsea.

United fell to seventh place in the league. It was another test of character for Ferguson's youthful side. Once again, they wouldn't be found wanting in their response.

United: Schmeichel, G Neville, Johnsen, May, Irwin, Cruyff, Beckham, Poborsky (Scholes), Butt, Solskjaer (Giggs), Cantona.

Liverpool: James, Bjornabye, Babb, Scales (Redknapp), Matteo, Thomas, McAteer, Berger, McManaman, Collymore, Barnes.

Attendance: 55, 128

19 April 1997

Liverpool 1 Manchester United 3

By the time we resumed our rivalry with Liverpool, the Reds were back at the top and well on the way to a fourth league title in five years, having put together an unbeaten run of sixteen games before a surprise reverse at Sunderland in March, followed by an even more surprising loss at home to Derby.

The United of 1996-97 could be erratic, but we had the character to shrug off those losses quickly as well as a manager who clearly demanded it in no uncertain terms. If these were attributes that our opponents in this game still lacked, Liverpool were beginning to convince people that they were on their way to putting it right. They'd led the league by five points at the turn of the year, leading to the inevitable recycling of phrases like 'Liverpool are back where they belong', 'Fortress Anfield' and 'vintage Liverpool' even though few could really remember what that was. They'd benefited from a more settled squad this season: their only expensive signing had been Patrick Berger, one of Poborsky's team mates from the Czech Republic team, while John Scales had been sold to Spurs, always a convenient dumping ground for expensive mistakes.

As the season went on, however, Liverpool began to fall away, their lack of true credentials exemplified when, on the day of United's loss to Derby, they failed to take advantage, losing at home to Coventry. While Liverpool had undoubtedly improved, there was a flakiness about them that left them short of the genuine article. The same was true of Newcastle and, when those two teams met in March, they played out a thrilling game that Sky Sports instantly proclaimed a classic, Liverpool eventually running out 4-3 winners. However, the game, while admittedly highly entertaining, was littered with defensive errors and illustrated the lack of substance within both pretenders to United's throne.

This match, sixteen days later, was a far more crucial fixture in determining the outcome of the championship. A win for United would effectively end the threat from Anfield, while a home victory would put Liverpool above the Reds with only three games to go. In the event, United fulfilled the expectations of most neutral observers by winning with something to spare. The Reds opened the scoring with a stunning header from Pallister at a corner, the defender putting right his error earlier in the first half when a careless pass had gifted a chance to

McManaman, only for the Liverpool player to fail to capitalise.

Liverpool's response also came from a header, veteran John Barnes rising in the area to score past Schmeichel, who got an arm to the ball but couldn't keep it out. The space Barnes had been allowed in the United box won't have pleased Ferguson, but as expected there were frequent examples of defensive frailty at the other end of the pitch and it was only a matter of time before United exploited them. Again it was Pallister who did it, rising at the near post from a corner earned after James had made a fine save to keep out Johnsen's header.

Despite doing well to thwart Johnsen's effort, James had clearly been at fault for the goal, coming off his line unnecessarily to allow Pally an unguarded target. By now the goalkeeper's weaknesses were well known. He once revealed he'd spend hours before a game relaxing by playing computer games, so perhaps his inexplicable advance off his line was caused by his desperation to deal with the large numbers of alien invaders that had followed United's players into his area and were dancing around menacingly before him. As it was, he'd succeeded only in punching in the head his colleague Wright, who might have looked like an alien invader but probably wasn't.

I'm not even sure that the presence of imaginary invaders could explain James' attempt to prevent United's third goal, if you could call it that. Gary Neville's speculative cross drifted apparently harmlessly to the far post and again, rather than allow his defence to deal with it, James followed its trajectory as if mesmerised, before flailing at some non-existent threat while Andy Cole was busy heading the ball back into his unprotected goal.

Television replays afterwards revealed Roy Evans reacting to his goalkeeper's error apparently by wafting a fart away from his nose. Was this was a misplaced attempt to locate the source of the problem? Or had panic resulting from his goalkeeper's antics caused him to follow through?

Admittedly, there was a sense this season of United stumbling towards the line largely because others were falling over more often that we were. We went on a run of three draws, coming from two goals down to salvage something at Leicester City before drawing 3-3 against Middlesbrough at Old Trafford. However, defeat at Wimbledon for Liverpool meant United still won the league with two games to spare. Having made a better job of our European campaign, United's run sadly ended with a disappointing semi-final defeat to eventual champions Borussia Dortmund.

There was certainly a case to be made for the view that other teams made it easy for United to retain the title that season. Even so, there was something very Liverpool FC about comments from Mark Wright, who insisted that, despite eventually limping home in fourth place, they'd been the league's best team, claiming that only poor goalkeeping from David James had prevented them from winning the title. [5] While James' poor goalkeeping had certainly played a part in the team's failure to finish higher in the league – this game being a prime example – it's very hard to make such a claim stick given that Liverpool had a better defensive record than both United and Newcastle over the season. Instead, Liverpool's goal tally of 62, sixteen short of United's haul, suggested that David James and his stash of computer games weren't the only problem.

Liverpool: James, Bjornabye, Wright, Harkness, Kvarme, McAteer (Collymore), Redknapp, McManaman, Thomas, Barnes (Berger), Fowler.

United: Schmeichel, G Neville, Johnsen, Pallister, P Neville, Butt, Scholes (McClair), Keane, Beckham, Cole, Cantona.

Attendance: 40,892

6 December 1997

Liverpool 1 Manchester United 3

The departure of Eric Cantona had been as sudden and unexpected as his arrival. Apparently he just decided he didn't want to play football anymore. Some have put it down to his disappointment over the defeat to Dortmund, which he took to have been a sign that success in European football would not be forthcoming for United any time soon (he was wrong, of course); others have noted that, following his extraordinary performances in 1995-96, Cantona, although still very good by anyone else's standards, hadn't been as impressive the following season and simply wanted to leave with the legend intact. Others simply stated the obvious – that this was the kind of guy Cantona was and he'd simply made the decision that felt right to him. Phillipe Auclair, in his excellent biography, has pointed to Cantona's regular trips to Paris when his team mates were on international breaks, mingling with arthouse directors and becoming actively involved in the Caargo theatre company. [6] For Auclair, his decision to retire was largely just a result of his interests shifting elsewhere. Admittedly that wasn't a very common reason for a footballer hanging up his boots, but then this was not your average footballer.

The early months of 1996-97 suggested United weren't missing him at all, although there would be times, as the season went on, where his absence was identified as the reason why United eventually fell short of expectations. Even an Eric Cantona not at his best had been a damn fine player and someone able to conjure something special at an unexpected moment. Later in the season, we'd be crying out for some of that. At the moment, however, the talk was of United moving effortlessly towards another league title. After we'd won this match, the bulk of the sports media looked at the fixture list to come over and after the Christmas period and talked of the championship race potentially being over by March.

It wouldn't work out like that, but for now the Reds were rampant while our opponents would experience another season of riding reasonably high in the league while never looking like getting close to the top two of United and Arsenal. Here, United took control in the second half, taking the lead with a clinical finish from Andy Cole. Although teenage prodigy Michael Owen won a penalty for Liverpool which Fowler dispatched, it proved a mere hiccup in United's onward march to the three points: a superb David Beckham free kick restored the lead before a wicked in-swinging corner from Giggs was headed on by Sheringham for Cole to grab his second at the far post. Cole's reputation as a profligate finisher was quickly fading: this was already his fifteenth goal of the season.

The result left United twelve points clear of Liverpool. It also meant that the free scoring Reds had now racked up a remarkable 27 goals in the last six games. We'd won five of those six, though the one defeat in that run - a 3-2 reverse at Arsenal – would sadly turn out to be by far the most significant when it came to determining the destination of the title.

Liverpool: James, Bjornabye (Riedle), Kvarme (Berger), Matteo, Carragher, McManaman, Redknapp, Leonhardsen, McAteer, Owen, Fowler.

United: Schmeichel, G Neville, Berg, Pallister, Johnsen, P Neville, Beckham, Butt, Giggs, Sheringham, Cole.

Attendance: 41,027

10 April 1998

Manchester United 1 Liverpool 1

Sadly, the optimism that had been so prevalent at the time of the last meeting between the sides had now been replaced by the grim prospect failure. Following that excellent first half of the season, the wheels had begun to fall off for United at the end of December when a shock defeat at Coventry had suddenly interrupted that apparent easy procession towards another league title. January defeats away at Southampton and at home to Leicester City had transformed an inconvenient hitch into something approaching genuine crisis. This poor run of form – which went on to include a shock defeat at Barnsley in the FA Cup – had allowed Arsenal to close the gap. When the Gunners came to Old Trafford in March and left with all three points they assumed control of the title race. It was a control that, in the weeks since, they hadn't shown any signs of letting slip.

Although United went into this game six points clear at the top, Arsenal had three games in hand and were in convincing form. They'd not conceded a goal in eight league games and were in the middle of a ten game winning streak that would include victory at home to Newcastle the day after this Good Friday game, which cut the gap and made the possibility of United finishing without a trophy for only the second time in nine season a very real one.

Although well out of the picture in third place, Liverpool fans were inevitably happy enough with the consolation of playing a small part in United failing to win the league. Tensions between the two sets of fans had been cranked up still further this season following the arrival at Anfield of Paul Ince, the former United midfielder who'd returned to England after two years at Inter Milan. Liverpool fans' eagerness to welcome Ince to the club was laughable: a player who'd always been detested and generally labelled as over-rated when at United was now hailed as a new saviour at Anfield. Needless to say, the move wasn't a popular one among United fans, for whom a move to a club's rivals was one of the few things that guaranteed something other than the customary warm welcome for former players. Given the circumstances surrounding his departure from Old Trafford, it was also inevitable that Ince would return to England with something to prove to his former boss.

Ince hadn't featured in the first game between the clubs that season, but now returned to Old Trafford in the colours of his former team's great rivals. This Paul Ince, however, was also proving to be a shadow of the player who'd shone in Ferguson's first great United side when, for a time, he only had his partner Roy Keane as a rival for the title of best midfielder in the country. Here, however, Ince appeared driven to ensure that his new club, despite being on the back foot for most of the game, didn't finish on the losing side.

A bruising encounter, with Ince and Liverpool doing much of the bruising, had nonetheless begun well for United when Ronny Johnsen opened the scoring in the twelfth minute, before an error from Gary Pallister – in what would turn out to be his last United-Liverpool game - let in Michael Owen for the equaliser. Perhaps the example of the fiery Ince had been taken on board rather too zealously by the teenager because he then began to set about his opponents' legs with as much ferocity as he'd struck the ball for his goal. He'd already been booked after following in on Schmeichel and, soon after the goal, he dived in on Johnsen with studs showing and was rightly sent off.

Predictably, United dominated the remainder of the game but the best we could produce was an Andy Cole effort that Rob Jones cleared off the line. Not for the first or last time, Liverpool left Old Trafford with a draw that, to them, must have felt very much like victory. For United, dropping points against ten men was clearly not the stuff of potential champions, and we knew it.

United: Schmeichel, G Neville, Irwin, Johnsen (May), Butt, Pallister, Beckham, P Neville (Sheringham), Cole, Scholes, Giggs (Thornley).

Liverpool: Friedel, Jones, Babb, Harkness, Matteo, McManaman, Leonhardsen, Redknapp, Ince, Murphy (Berger), Owen.

Attendance: 55,171

Performance record (Ferguson v Evans)*

Games – 10
United wins – 6
Draws – 2
Liverpool wins - 2

Honours during Ferguson-Evans period

Manchester United – 3 Premier Leagues; 2 FA Cups; 3 FA Charity Shields
Liverpool – 1 League Cup

Transfer expenditure during Ferguson-Evans period

Incoming transfers
Manchester United – £27.35 million
Liverpool – £43.1 million

Outgoing transfers
Manchester United – £28.22 million
Liverpool – £15.45 million

Net spend
Manchester United – -£0.87 million
Liverpool – £27.65 million

*The one United-Liverpool game that occurred during the joint management period of Evans and Houllier has been included in the statistics for Houllier.

References

1. Press Association article – available at
www.lfchistory.net/Articles/Article/775
2. A. Ferguson, Leading, p106
3. **www.lfchistory.net/Transfers**
4. **www.wsc.co.uk/wsc-daily/979-January-2010/4418-business-as-usual-**

for-the-birmingham-three
5.https://en.wikipedia.org/wiki/1996%E2%80%9397_Liverpool_F.C._season#cite_note-5
6. P Auclair, Cantona, p452

4

Make Mine a Treble

Ferguson v Houllier

24 September 1998

Manchester United 2 Liverpool 0

It was, of course, hard for anyone to anticipate just what lay ahead for United that season although I would, one glorious night in May, find myself in a local pub standing next to a milkman who'd put money on United to win the treble early in the campaign and was, inevitably, celebrating even more loudly than everyone else. The season had begun rather differently, and with the ABUs in full voice. Not only had Arsenal taken our championship, but England had suffered their customary disappointment in the World Cup and those embarking on their four-yearly search for a scapegoat had found one neatly giftwrapped in United colours.

The national embarrassment that was the vilification of David Beckham was at full tilt. Beckham was being viciously hounded by the British press and away supporters all over the country after being blamed for England's defeat to Argentina. Many Liverpool supporters, who a decade ago were declaring themselves unconcerned with the fate of the national team, of course joined in, happy to align themselves with any campaign that had United on the receiving end.

United, particularly those sides managed by Ferguson, always responded well when the world was against us, of course, and the season's early games, with anti-Beckham fervour at its peak, would simply raise the intensity at the beginning of the greatest rollercoaster ride of a season experienced by any English side, ever. Did the jeers and efigee-burning help to motivate us in our pursuit of what had once seemed impossible? You can bet that Fergie, a master motivator with that skill all truly great managers have for turning problems into opportunities, would have made use of it.

There were certainly big challenges ahead. Arsenal had showed last season that, unlike Newcastle or Blackburn, they had enough about them to give United a run for their money over more than just one campaign. With the names of potential big signings being bandied about all summer – Argentina's Gabriel Batistuta being probably the most popular among United fans – there had been some consternation when the club eventually brought in Dwight Yorke from Aston Villa.

The move was apparently unwelcome in all quarters, Villa manager John Gregory declaring 'If I'd had a gun I'd have shot him,' when Yorke informed him of his desire to leave. Fanzine United We Stand would, in the coming months, devote a full page to a picture of the player with the caption 'Dwight Yorke – Some of Us Owe You a Big Apology' when the striker proved an instant success. His easy-going nature and apparently permanent smile alleviated much of the gloom hanging over Old Trafford from the previous campaign and from an early stage he combined brilliantly with Andy Cole to form easily the most devastating strike partnership in England and, it would later turn out, the whole of Europe.

There had been a much more positive greeting from fans for giant Dutch defender Jaap Stam, arriving to fill the gap left by the departure of Gary Pallister, while winger Jesper Blomqvist had also arrived to provide back-up on the wings. Another veteran, Brian McClair, one of Fergie's first signings, finally called time on another of the truly great United careers. He would subsequently join the club's academy staff, his association with the club continuing until the summer of 2015.

The season had started slowly, to say the least, and United went into this game back in tenth place, following an ominous 3-0 defeat at Arsenal that suggested the Gunners had no intention of letting their grip on the title slip despite making a fitful start to the season themselves. Before that United had been involved in unconvincing draws at home to Leicester and away at West Ham, with only a crushing defeat of Charlton Athletic – in which Yorke starred – giving any hint of what was to come.

Meanwhile, Liverpool were once again in transition. Despite getting closer to the league title under Roy Evans than they'd managed since the Dalglish era, they decided they'd have a chance of getting even closer if they gave Evans a friend to work with. Gerard Houllier, the former French manager who'd been instrumental in Eric Cantona joining United, was duly brought in. Apparently Evans wasn't too happy with this arrangement: this would prove to be his final United-Liverpool game before he decided to leave the club in November.

Coming only four days after the disappointment of defeat at Arsenal and with Liverpool knowing victory here would put them top of the table, United really needed a win and a convincing performance and we got both. Admittedly we were helped by Brad Friedel following in the welcome traditions set by Grobbelaar and James of producing woeful goalkeeping displays at Old Trafford. He certainly made an important contribution to United's opener, struggling to deal with Solksjaer's shot and allowing the ball to slip away for a corner which he then failed to clear. The ball fell to Scholes in the area and, when that happened, there was usually only one result. McAteer apparently decided he'd rather his keeper take his chances from twelve yards than allow Scholesy to shoot. Irwin stepped up to take the resulting penalty and made no mistake.

From there it was easy, the only serious threat dealt with ably by Schmeichel who showed Friedel how it was done when he made a brilliant save from Redknapp's free kick look easy. Other than that, it was pretty much one-way traffic and United eventually sealed the game with Scholes' long-range effort eleven minutes from time. The win lifted United to fifth place and set off a run of only one win in six games that would see Liverpool's early challenge fall away, effectively once again putting them out of contention and setting the scene for Roy Evans to go out with things pretty much the same as when he came in.

United: Schmeichel, P Neville, Stam, G Neville, Irwin, Beckham, Keane, Scholes (Butt), Giggs, Yorke, Solskjaer (Cole).

Liverpool: Friedel, McAteer, Carragher, Babb, Bjornabye, McManaman, Redknapp, Ince, Berger, Riedle (Fowler), Owen.

Attendance: 55,181

24 January 1999

FA Cup Round Four

Manchester United 2 Liverpool 1

You never know how things will turn out, of course, but during the second half of this season things happened that left the strong impression that something really special might be on the cards. Things like the comeback at Juventus, Schmeichel's penalty save from Bergkamp before Giggy's extra time winner against Arsenal and this, a victory that, to follow the cliché, was truly snatched from the jaws of defeat against a Liverpool side whose devastation at the end was gratifyingly apparent. They'd thought they'd done enough, their faces said. But there was never any such thing against a United side that simply didn't give up, ever.

To achieve what United did that season unquestionably required more than just talented players; it needed not just a team spirit but a squad spirit, that demanded, for instance, that the likes of Ole Gunnar Solskjaer didn't despair when playing second fiddle to the brilliantly in-form Yorke and Cole, and instead to seize opportunities when they came. And it needed the absolute conviction to believe that you weren't beaten even though all the signs were pointing in that direction: United would not have pulled off their remarkable trophy haul that season had a single player in the team felt 'well that's it' or 'our name's not on it' when the chips were down. Here with two minutes left, Liverpool weren't only winning but looked to have survived the barrage United had thrown at them. Against any other team in the world that year, that might have been enough.

Overall, this was hardly a vintage performance from United. Poor defending led to Liverpool taking the lead in only the third minute, an unmarked Michael Owen given the freedom of the penalty area in front of the Stretford End to open the scoring with a well-placed header. But this United team, even when not at their scintillating best, still managed to create chances. There were three near misses for Roy Keane, the first when his header back across the goal was scrambled off the goal line; a fierce second half shot from the Irishman was later deflected narrowly wide; finally, he struck the post when he'd looked certain to score

Again, many sides would have dropped their heads at this point, but the 1998-99 United side were not among them. The Cole-Yorke combination brought United level with only two minutes remaining, a header across the area from the former finding his strike partner, who tapped in from close range. That season, it was as if the board being raised by the fourth official was taken as a personal message by Ole Gunnar Solskjaer to indicate how much time he had left to influence proceedings. When the substitute received the ball in the box, there really was only one result and that was a bulge in the back of the Liverpool net and rampant celebrations in the Stretford End.

Of course, the ABUs regarded such late shows as evidence of nothing other than luck favouring United. Those who raised such objections didn't, of course, find themselves in the presence of winners in the way we did and therefore might be excused their ignorance, if we were feeling charitable. When that charge was levelled at South African golfer Gary Player, who had the temerity to be a frequent winner of golf tournaments on US soil, he replied, 'It's funny – the harder I work, the luckier I get.' United players clearly possessed a similar drive not simply to exploit fortune but to guide its hand through sheer will. And like Player, criticism from the supporters of others just added to our determination to rub their noses in it. Plus there was the influence of a Scottish bloke on the sidelines who was kicking and heading every ball with you and who would have something to say if anything at all was left on the pitch at the end.

United: Schmeichel, G Neville (Solskjaer), Berg (Johnsen), Stam, Irwin, Keane, Giggs, Beckham, Butt (Scholes), Yorke, Cole.

Liverpool: James, Heggem, Harkness, Bjornabye, Carragher, Matteo, Berger, Ince (McAteer), Redknapp, Owen, Fowler.

Attendance: 54,591

5 May 1999

Liverpool 2 Manchester United 2

'This was our Cup Final,' slobbered a Liverpool fan to me the following morning. 'We stopped you winning the league. That's our Cup Final, that. Now you'll win fuck all.'

His elegantly expressed verdict betrayed at least two things about the body of people he represented. Firstly, that supporters of Liverpool FC had long abandoned the dignified pursuit of honours, replaced only by that fear of a red planet that had hung so brightly over them through the Roy Evans era. It left the desperate need to see United fail whatever and whoever it took lest their worst nightmare, which had already lasted a good six years, should continue its stranglehold over whatever sleeping patterns they still had left. Secondly, they still seriously underestimated United's ability to bounce back from setbacks, and certainly setbacks as minor as this one.

Admittedly, at the time the result of this game looked to have given Arsenal a chance to snatch the title from us. It left United second in the league, Arsenal having defeated Spurs on the same night. They were on 75 points with two games to play, while United stood on 72 with an additional game left.   Goal difference was close and could still go either way, so Liverpool supporters' belief that they had dealt a serious blow to United's title hopes was understandable, if highly premature.   The unspoken fear that lay behind such bravado, of course, came with the knowledge that, had United won this game, it would have made things far easier for the Reds in what remained of the season. Having blown their own shot at the treble at United's hands way back in 1977, it was unthinkable for Liverpool fans that United should now go on to complete it. But the unthinkable can happen, as they were about to find out.

The stakes had, it was true, been raised before the game by Fergie, not for the first time. It said much for Liverpool supporters' proclivity for making mountains out of molehills, however, that Fergie's labelling of his former player Paul Ince as a 'Big Time Charlie' had been seized upon quite so zealously. A Leeds fan I know couldn't fathom out the reason for the offence. 'Is there something about that phrase I'm not getting?' he asked me. 'Racist or something?' No, merely a label used by Ferguson to remind his players of Incey's desire to be a big-shot and that he was likely to try to use the occasion of a game against United to that effect. He was using his knowledge and experience to alert his players to a player on the opposition, warning them not to be wound up by him. Liverpool fans took offence. Some birds went tweet.

Enhanced by its importance in the race for the league title, and the pre-match hype that arose from Fergie's remark, this Wednesday night game at Anfield was one of those Liverpool-United encounters that oozed tension, the implications of the result going well beyond the match itself and, during the second half, having that apparent time-suspending, almost other-worldly element that games like this have about them. It seemed to last about four hours.

United took the game to Liverpool from the off, Dwight Yorke's far post header to meet a trademark Beckham cross from the right giving the Reds the lead in front of the Kop. We doubled the lead in the second half after Sheringham's run had been unfairly cut off in the Liverpool area by Carragher and Denis Irwin scored from the spot. At that point there appeared, temporarily, a sense of mission accomplished; instead, the game appeared to spin off into some other footballing realm with its own sense of time and its own rules. Those other rules were something referee David Ellary clearly felt drawn into. An innocuous looking tackle by Jesper Blomqvist – a player very much of the Jesper Olsen school of struggling to punch a hole in a wet paper bag – brought a penalty to Liverpool and, when Redknapp converted it, an unlikely opportunity to get back into the game.

There followed one of the most ludicrous decisions every seen in the history of this fixture, or indeed any other fixture. Irwin was making his way up the left touchline when the linesman's flag went up to signal the ball had gone out of play. Irwin, one of the most honest professionals ever to wear a football shirt, stopped and passed the ball infield only to find that the ref had interpreted his act as kicking it away, a judgement that appeared to astonish players on both sides. Already on a yellow, this meant a sending off for the left-back. It meant, of course, that United now had to negotiate the remainder of this high-octane contest with ten men. It also meant Irwin would be suspended for the FA Cup Final.

United were clearly rattled by the decision and Liverpool took full advantage. It seemed almost inevitable, given the game's immediate pre-history and way the night's events had turned, that Ince should grab the equaliser, celebrating with the Kop as if the goal had won the Premier League, Boat Race, Eurovision Song Contest and Crufts rather than simply applying a mild dent to his former side's championship hopes. There was only a minute left on the clock, leaving a distinctly hollow ring to Liverpool supporters' allegations of luck when United had had the temerity to score late on against them in our previous encounter. Now they went into wild spasms of ecstasy, something that they'd once reserved for famous European victories but which now accompanied the apparently almost sexual thrill they experienced on drawing at home to United.

Ince, clearly hell bent on demolishing what remained of his reputation among United fans, ran to the other end cupping his hand to his right ear. Perhaps surprisingly, I spoke to many Liverpool fans afterwards who told me they were disappointed by his gesture: celebrating in front of the Kop after his goal had been the right thing to do, but his second response suggested – as did the fact that he had been so unusually fired up throughout the game – that putting one over his former team and manager meant far more to him than playing for Liverpool. Had he signed for them simply for the opportunity to piss Fergie off in the best possible way? Having failed to apply anything like the level of intensity seen here during the rest of his time with Liverpool, he would leave the club in the close season.

In the event, this result proved merely a minor hitch to United, something that simply added extra spice to the most memorable of run ins ever; it might even have pumped up the Reds still further in their pursuit of that incredible treble. United won 1-0 at Middlesbrough the following weekend to keep the title race on a knife edge and ensure that goal difference remained too close to call. However, on the Monday night, Reds had a rare reason to celebrate along with our other deadly rivals Leeds when the Yorkshire club pulled off an unexpected win against Arsenal. It meant the Reds only required a win and a draw from their final two matches to win the league. A goalless draw at Blackburn in midweek was duly followed by victory over Spurs on the last day to give United the championship, Liverpool running in a pitiful seventh.

And of course that wasn't the end of the season for United; far from it. Looking back, although there were several moments when it looked like we might have we'd blown it, including during the Champions League Final itself, the whole experience now just feels like a heady ten days of celebration, not just in terms of the trophies won, but simply to have lived to see and support a United side like that one of 1998-99. It was, simply, the best of times and even setbacks like the one that night in Anfield in the end coalesced into a series of events that were, and remain, utterly unforgettable.

Liverpool: Friedel, Staunton (Thompson), Song (Berger), Babb, Carragher, Matteo, Leonhardsen, McManaman, Ince, Redknapp, Riedle.

United: Schmeichel, G Neville, Johnsen, Stam, Irwin, Keane, Blomqvist (P Neville), Scholes, Beckham, Yorke, Cole (Butt).

Attendance: 44,712

11 September 1999

Liverpool 2 Manchester United 3

How do you top that? Much as the glorious memory of winning the Treble will remain with me, as it will all other Reds, for the rest of my life, in some ways it cast a shadow over the the triumphs that came our way over the next two years. The next two Premier League campaigns saw the league title returning again to Old Trafford – the first time we'd won it three times on the trot - and yet a failure to repeat our success in Europe meant the celebrations were tempered with a feeling that we were falling short of our full potential.

If that sounds to outsiders like we'd become a bit spoilt, then I agree, at least to an extent. Although, like other grounds, Old Trafford's atmosphere had been diluted already following the introduction of all-seated stadia, it unquestionably began to hit new depths of sterility in the years that followed the Treble victory. While many have put that down to the increased presence of day trippers and tourists in the expanded stadium, they can hardly carry the blame when the vast majority of those inside Old Trafford were, and still are, season ticket holders. Roy Keane would be right to criticise the 'prawn sandwich brigade' for the declining match day atmosphere, but too many assumed he was referring only to those casual supporters when in truth his criticisms were relevant to a large proportion of the home crowd, literal prawn sandwich munchers or not. On the other hand, whilst it's perfectly true that we *had* been spoilt by success, beyond most of our wildest dreams, it wasn't the whole story. Part of the problem was that looking down from a very high place can be a very scary thing.

Although the majority of Liverpool fans won't admit it, something similar happened to the Kop in the eighties. Their long period of success led to a gradually diminishing atmosphere. Although undoubtedly part of this was, as with Old Trafford later, due to fans familiar with watching successful sides simply feeling they could sit back and watch it happen without the effort of getting involved, it also had something to do with fear. Look again at the TV pictures of the Kop during that last gasp championship loss to Arsenal in 1989. The majority of faces are not beaming with joyful anticipation, but wracked with fear over what might happen, and this long before Arsenal looked capable of doing what they eventually did. Contrast that with supporters of a lower league team one-nil up against a Premiership club – their joy may well turn out to be short-lived, but they're determined to indulge in it while they can.

Once we've reached the top, whether we admit it or not, increasingly within us there lurks a fear of what will happen when it comes to an end. Not everyone inside Old Trafford or Anfield would have this concern at the forefront of their minds, but it lurks there like some unborn monster-child and it generates an atmosphere of nervous tension, whose more immediate offspring is a wave of silence that spreads to all corners of the ground.

Another thing that hung over the honeymoon period after the Treble was the club walking headlong into what many regarded at the time as a piece of bungled PR, but was actually something far worse. As European champions, United were invited to represent Europe in FIFA's new World Club Championship in Brazil. Unfortunately, the competition was to take place at the same time as the Third Round of the FA Cup. With England embarking on a predictably unsuccessful bid to stage the World Cup, the FA were keen for United to take part in order not to piss FIFA off and they duly asked the club to withdraw from the FA Cup and play in that tinpot competition instead. Silly them. Didn't they realise they'd have been better off keeping United at home and focusing their energies on stuffing suitcases with batches of used notes, giving them to high class prostitutes and packing them off to hotel rooms containing FIFA delegates?

The FA's insane determination to believe FIFA might actually award a World Cup to a country for football-related reasons resulted in a no-win situation for United. Had the club refused, they would surely have had the blame for England not getting the World Cup pinned on them. When the club agreed, they were vilified in all quarters for showing such contempt for a historic competition. The FA simply stood by and let United take the flak.

It was something we should never have allowed to happen. From the campaign for a player's union in the early years of the twentieth century to participation in Europe in the fifties, an important part of United's identity has always been a refusal to kow-tow to the demands of British football's authorities. Here, we learned the hard way what happened when we went along with them. Not only did we sacrifice a very important part of the club's soul and go against the wishes of our own fans who preferred defence of the FA Cup to participation in a meaningless international competition any day, we learned what we should have known already: that Manchester United make very convenient scapegoats.

Throughout our history, United had consistently taken English football in the right direction whether the game's authorities agreed with our approach or not. This time, we allowed the game's authorities to lead us even against the preferred direction of our own supporters, and the results were predictably bad for everyone: England didn't get to host the World Cup and United exchanged defence of a competition that had brought so many of the most memorable moments in that most memorable of seasons for a meaningless couple of weeks in Brazil.

The situation was yet another symptom of the different priorities of the corporate giant that was the modern Manchester United and the club beloved of its supporters. They'd been more apparent than ever during the previous season when, following Rupert Murdoch's attempt to seize control of the club, hardcore Reds had won what had initially seemed an unlikely victory to keep United from the hands of the media mogul. At the start, few had given us a prayer, but the victorious campaign showed that a well-organised group of football supporters could take on even the most powerful of businessmen and win, when there was a will to do so and a cause to fight for. Although this was not the first time supporters of a football club had mobilised to defend their interests against the club's board, it was the first time the supporters of a truly high profile club had done so, and done so in such a well-organised way.

Not only that, but these were not protests against owners looking to sell off the ground, or move the club from its base in the manner of the shameful Wimbledon/Milton Keynes scenario, or asset-strip it into financial oblivion. As many pointed out, the Murdoch takeover would have actually given United still greater financial clout. The truth was that, when it came down to it, hardcore United fans cared about something more than that. The club's soul was at stake and, even though their actions couldn't prevent the Malcolm Glazer takeover a few years later, it was a display of solidarity with the club's working class and community origins that, you suspect, few on the board understood let alone empathised with. It was telling that, when the takeover of Manchester city by an oil-rich sheikh occurred a few years later, the welcome mat was laid before them pretty much unanimously by city fans. They'd spent years castigating United fans for allegedly buying success, yet when there was a chance to defend their club from a tsunami of filthy lucre heading their way, instead they'd leapt in and taken a bath in it.

Meanwhile, Liverpool had once again been busy in the transfer market, quietly moving the last bunch of players who'd been set to take the world by storm, honest, out of Anfield to replace them with another lot. Their brief dalliance with Paul Ince had ended in tears, his departure coming mere months after his histrionics in the United game. Whether Houllier had figured out that he was, after all, a Big Time Charlie, was never placed on record but, needless to say, he left without having added to the medal collection he'd amassed at United. Another new central defensive partnership – this time consisting of Hyypia and Henchoz – was introduced and David James made way in goal for new arrival Sandor Westerveld. Short-lived flavour of the month Titi Camara arrived in attack as did another Czech international, the almost unfeasibly lightweight Vladimir Smicer. An enormous eight million quid was lavished on German midfielder Dietmar Hamann. There was, inevitably, much wailing and gnashing of teeth when the home-produced Steve McManaman let his contract run down and fucked off to Real Madrid without the club receiving a penny. In total, thirteen players left the club that summer, including the once much-lauded Rob Jones, who departed on a free transfer to West Ham, and Karl-Heinz Riedle, who'd arrived as a Champions League winner from Dortmund, but now went to Fulham for a mere £200,000.

On the field, needless to say, it remained one-way traffic in United's direction. In the league, United began where the previous season had left off and looked pretty much irresistible from the word go. The Reds went into this game unbeaten and top of the league, a situation that would persist until the shock of a 5-0 reverse at Chelsea in October. It would prove a temporary hitch, one of only three defeats in the league that season.

One thing that United were finding difficult, as many had anticipated, was replacing Peter Schmeichel, who'd announced his intention to leave the club at the beginning of the 1998-99 season and duly departed on the highest possible note, having replaced the absent Roy Keane to captain the side on that famous night in Barcelona. The Reds had secured the return of Mark Bosnich, who'd enjoyed a brief spell with United at the end of the eighties, from Aston Villa, but he was already looking unconvincing. Fergie, indeed, would place on record his regrets regarding the signing, a deal having been agreed by the United board without him knowing it as he went off in pursuit of Edwin Van der Sar, who of course would later go on to be an enormous success at the club. Apparently the area in which Bosnich made most of an impact was at the dinner table:

his new boss clearly wasn't too impressed at his ability to guzzle multiple meals in one sitting, although you do wonder what kind of plummeting sales local fast food outlets suffered after his release: Anderson's arrival, after all, was still some years away. [1] It's testimony to the sheer attacking quality of the Reds that season that we would win the league so convincingly without a truly first class goalkeeper.

With the jury out (to lunch, perhaps) over the future of Bosnich, the scene was set for the figure of Massimo Taibi and one of the most bizarre cameos in United's history. Signed from Italian club Venezia for £4.5 at the end of August, Taibi arrived amid a fanfare of optimism but he would ultimately prove the most infamous symbol of the club's failure to replace Schmeichel convincingly in the years before Van Der Sar finally arrived in 2005. It's not so much that Taibi was rubbish, rather that he was erratic to the point of making the defence in front of him foul their shorts whenever opponents got anywhere near the penalty area. His debut came in this match.

Taibi contributed in various ways to a highly entertaining spectacle and, against the keeper's later reputation (much deserved, it has to be said) as an expensive mistake should be set the decision of Sky Sports to name him man of the match for his performance here. Yet, while it was true he made some fine saves, he also looked twitchy throughout and there was a deep sense even then that on another day he might not get away with it. Sadly, it wasn't long before that day arrived. Incidentally, alongside Taibi, Mikael Silvestre also made his United debut here following his arrival from Internazionale, while making his first appearance in a Liverpool-United clash was a young Steven Gerrard.

Liverpool were ninth going into this game but, as usual, an unexpected win against Arsenal in their previous outing had left many of their supporters confident that world domination was just around the corner and that the Rubicon moment would come with them ending a long run of poor results against United. The opening goal suggested their defence were in far too generous a mood to pull it off, however. Giggs's cross from the left was met by Carragher at the near post and the Liverpool defender managed to produce a stunning glancing header to beat Westerveld in only the third minute.

United went two up when Beckham's excellent free kick on the right was met with a firm header from Andy Cole that deflected in off the keeper. Unfortunately, the two goal cushion was short lived as Taibi then decided to start his United career in earnest. The keeper came off his line needlessly to flail at a long Liverpool free kick, allowing Hyypia to sneak in behind him and head into the empty net.

Following the error, United's defence immediately began to look shaky. At the other end, however, our rivals' back four were clearly determined not to be upstaged and, when another Beckham free kick from the right came in, Song grabbed a handful of Cole's shirt to drag the United forward out of the way and allow space for Carragher once again to bundle the ball into his own goal.

Cole missed a glorious chance early in the second half that would probably have seen United go on to win comfortably. As it was, Liverpool produced a sustained onslaught to set the stage for Taibi's all too brief period of glory in United colours. He made a fine reflex save to deny Smicer then saved with his legs to deflect wide Fowler's header from the resulting corner. Another near post save denied the latter again before Berger reduced United's lead after beating the offside trap to stroke the ball past Taibi, who on this occasion had no chance.

Hopes were raised further among Liverpool fans when Cole reacted to a challenge from Song, who'd been niggling at him throughout the game, with a flurry of arms and a kick out at the Cameroon defender that brought a second yellow card and a dismissal. Taibi had to be alert again to get his body in the way and ensure a Michael Owen shot trickled wide of his near post, but it was Liverpool's last meaningful chance and the Reds held out to win. In the context of the rest of his United career – which totalled only five games – it would be the United keeper's wild flail at the cross that led to Liverpool's first goal that would be most remembered. However, this was a decisive and probably match-winning performance from a keeper who, if nothing else, had left his mark at Anfield as a United player. Few among the United support would have liked to risk a repeat performance, however, and we wouldn't have to: by the end of the season, Taibi would be back in Italy.

Liverpool: Westerveld, Song, Hyypia, Matteo, Carragher, Berger, Gerrard (Heggem), Thompson (Smicer), Redknapp, Camara (Owen), Fowler.

United: Taibi, Silvestre, Berg, Stam, P Neville (Clegg), Scholes, Beckham, Giggs, Butt (Wallwork), Yorke, Cole.

Attendance: 44, 929

4 March 2000

Manchester United 1 Liverpool 1

The whole FIFA Club World Championship fiasco had ended in, well, fiasco, as a clearly indifferent United bowed out in the group stage to Mexican side Necaxa. Preceding them on their flight out were ABU cries about how the club were going to shaft English football further using the trip to make millions out of a merchandising and diplomacy exercise. Then, when that didn't happen and the Reds instead locked themselves away in a training camp, they were accused of ruining the lives of expectant Brazilian youngsters. Rival clubs waded in with accusations that the club had been awarded an effective mid-season break complete with the benefits of warm weather training.

Needless to say, none of that bothered Alex Ferguson. Hopefully it was a lesson for the club, though, that a Manchester United so dominant over the English game were never going to make friends and that, in trying, it would only ever make things worse and bring the club no benefits whatsoever. The mid-season break accusation was a joke, of course. It was clear by that stage that United were going to win the league anyway, eventually doing so by an almost ludicrous margin of eighteen points.

On the way, we would dish out some severe hammerings, beating Bradford City 4-0 home and away before celebrating with them on the last day of the season when they triumphed over Liverpool to save themselves from relegation and, in the process, deny their opponents a Champions League place. The away victory came in a run of eight games between March and May in which the Reds scored three times in each, 31 goals coming from the run with the highlight a 7-1 demolition of West Ham.

Living, as they do, in their own peculiar dreamland, Liverpool still felt going into this game that a ten point gap between the clubs could be overturned, with the prospect of a Champions League place viewed with expectation rather than hope at that point, particularly as they'd again come off a win against Arsenal, this time away from home.

Their optimism was cranked up a further notch when they opened the scoring, admittedly in some style, in the twenty-seventh minute, Berger's left-footed strike thirty yards out flying past Van der Gouw who, though in his fourth season at Old Trafford, was playing in his first ever United-

Liverpool game. It looked likely that Liverpool would take the lead into the break but, just before half-time, Solskjaer latched onto a Giggs cross from the left and steered it through the legs of Henchoz for the equalizer. A frantic second half failed to produce any more goals and the game finished with honours even. These were to prove the last points United dropped that season, the last eleven league games all ending in victory.

The league was effectively in the bag by the time we faced quarter-final opponents Real Madrid in the Champions League. Even so, the disappointment of losing that left a sour feeling for the remainder of the season, especially as a goalless game at the Bernabeu in the first leg had brought so much optimism. A much improved Real Madrid turned up for the second leg, beating United 3-2 and leaving only that procession of largely routine league fixtures to fulfil, the fact that the Reds performed so well in them only adding to the sense of what might have been. Again, the fact that we ended a season in which we'd dominated the Premier League so comprehensively in a mood of disappointment said much about our collective psyche at that time as well as the level of expectation engendered by that treble triumph. Bradford's last day victory would probably give us more satisfaction than any of those wins of our own.

United: Van der Gouw, G Neville, Stam, Silvestre, Irwin, Beckham, Keane, Butt, Giggs, Yorke (Sheringham), Solskjaer (Cole).

Liverpool: Westerveld, Heggem (Song), Henchoz, Hyypia (Murphy), Matteo, Smicer, Hamann, Carragher, Berger, Meijer, Camara (Owen).

Attendance: 61,592

17 December 2000

Manchester United 0 Liverpool 1

Another season and, even at this stage, we could anticipate another easy procession to another title. We'd led the table pretty much interrupted since 5 September, spending just a week in second place following our only defeat of the season so far, a 1-0 loss at Arsenal.

However, an expanding and still increasingly silent Old Trafford seemed even more listless. Although the league position and scorelines were satisfying, there was a sense of inertia about a team who, after securing the services of Fabien Barthez in yet another attempt to replace Schmeichel, added no further new faces in the summer and were progressing through a punishing two group stage in the new-look Champions League only as runners-up in both groups, first to Anderlecht and then to Valencia. We made the second group stage by the skin of our teeth, suffering two defeats and squeezing through in the last home game against Dynamo Kiev only as a result of the visitors spurning a golden chance to equalise late in the game.

Liverpool, meanwhile, were suddenly enjoying themselves. Gerard Houllier continued to carry out his overhaul of the playing squad and, for the first time in years, the work had the appearance of more than simply shovelling shit from one place to another. Mediocrities like Babb, Bjornabye, Matteo and Song were shown the door, while Titi Camara moved to West Ham United having failed to build on an initial promise that no one outside Anfield had felt was there anyway. Although some less than inspiring signings came in to replace them, there were some very shrewd investments, including the capture of Jari Litmanen from Barcelona on a free transfer and Gary McAllister, veteran of the 1992 Leeds championship side. McAllister was knocking on a bit but he proved a very wise short-term acquisition, adding intelligence and tactical awareness to a midfield that had lacked it for years. He would be used sparingly, and indeed wouldn't start in either of the United games during that campaign, but his presence over the season would prove invaluable. Houllier fielded five players making their United-Liverpool debut here, with Ferguson selecting another four, making this the second time in a year that the game had featured nine fixture debutants.

Although the league would prove to be well beyond them, Liverpool were already looking good value for a top three position that would secure them a place in the Champions League for the first time since the competition was revamped in the nineties. They'd also served notice of a serious tilt at a domestic cup triumph, dismissing Chelsea, Stoke (with an 8-0 thumping) and Fulham in the League Cup to secure what looked an extremely winnable semi-final meeting with Crystal Palace. Meanwhile, their UEFA Cup campaign was also going well, with progress to the last sixteen already secured.

Despite United's eminent league position, Liverpool probably went into this game with their confidence higher than that of their hosts for the first time in years. The game followed that pattern too and was settled by a single Danny Murphy goal just before half time. Gary Neville appeared almost to have to contort himself to handle the ball and give away the crucial free kick, but handle it he did and Murphy placed his shot just inside the right post of Barthez (who, incidentally, was the fourth different goalkeeper to feature for the Reds in as many United-Liverpool matches) to give Liverpool what was inevitably a boisterously celebrated victory. A red card for Luke Chadwick, who'd only been on the pitch for nine minutes, added to a disappointing day for the Reds.

United: Barthez, G Neville, Silvestre, Brown, Irwin (Chadwick), Beckham, Keane, Giggs, Butt (Greening), Scholes, Solskjaer.

Liverpool: Westerveld, Babbel, Hyypia, Henchoz, Carragher, Murphy (McAllister), Biscan, Gerrard, Barmby, Owen (Smicer), Heskey.

Attendance: 67,533

31 March 2001

Liverpool 2 Manchester United 0

Liverpool hadn't completed a league double over United since 1979-80, so you can imagine the scale of the celebrations that greeted this victory. The Reds hadn't lost in the league since the home defeat to Liverpool and had been on a good run of form, including a 6-1 demolition of Arsenal. From another perspective, however, such a comprehensive walloping of the side who would again be runners-up emphasised the poor quality of the domestic competition. Before that, a game against Everton had ended in a 1-0 win despite the Reds not recording a single shot on target, the winner coming from a Watson own goal. We were cruising to a league title while looking anything but convincing European challengers, where we regularly encountered opponents far less likely to lie back and be ravaged quite so easily.

The same applied when United were pitted against rare domestic rivals infused with a bit more spirit and a few long-lasting sores that required healing. Liverpool were feeling better about life than they had for more than a decade, and against them the Reds once again came unstuck. They already had the League Cup under their belts and looked forward with understandable optimism to a semi-final date with Wycombe Wanderers in the FA Cup. They'd seen off tricky opposition in the form of Porto and Roma (albeit via a bizarre and ultimately crucial change of mind by the referee on a penalty decision) and were anticipating with some relish a semi-final with Barcelona in the UEFA Cup. If we were comforting ourselves that this would surely be the point at which their European run would come to an inglorious end, we would be proved wrong. United were moving effortlessly towards another league title, but there was a feeling that, for once, Liverpool were enjoying life a lot more than we were.

In this game, our rivals played with the confidence of a side heading for multiple trophies for the first time since the glory days of the eighties, while United looked a million miles from the team that had thrashed Arsenal. Gerrard opened the scoring in the first half, crashing a long range shot past Barthez. Then, four minutes from half-time, Heskey's chip from the right found Fowler in the area. With Gary Neville falling over behind him, he smashed his shot into the roof of the net.

Although Danny Murphy was sent off in the 69th minute, United never looked like finding a way back into the game. We would win the league, of course, stumbling through the final games once the title had been sealed to finish the season with three defeats, a far cry from the triumphant surge over the line of the previous year. Liverpool went on to defeat both Wycombe and Barcelona and win both competitions, leading to a 'treble' of sorts that their fans knew wasn't actually the real thing but, being Liverpool fans, they proclaimed it as such anyway.

Liverpool: Westerveld, Babbel, Henchoz, Hyypia, Carragher, Berger (Barmby), Murphy, Hamann, Gerrard (Owen), Fowler (McAllister), Heskey.

United: Barthez, G Neville, Brown, Irwin (Chadwick), P Neville, Giggs, Beckham, Keane, Butt (Scholes), Yorke, Sheringham (Silvestre).

Attendance: 44,806

12 August 2001

FA Charity Shield

Liverpool 2 Manchester United 1

After this win at the Millennium Stadium, Liverpool fans now predictably claimed they'd completed the quadruple. The claim was both hilarious and depressing, a reminder of what kind of nonsense we'd have to put up with if they really were on the way back, something that was only further emphasised when victory in the Super Cup was transformed by those Merseyside spin doctors into a Quintuple (at least among those who knew the word existed). Just as concerning for United fans was the feeling that, despite those three consecutive titles, the clubs were roughly running neck and neck in terms of quality for the first time in the Premier League years. While United had been coasting to those titles, it seemed other parts of the English football world had quietly begun to catch up.

Even though the Reds had long ceased to regard this traditional curtain raiser as anything other than a glorified pre-season friendly, it was still hard not to conclude that the defeat offered further evidence Liverpool's improvement (albeit characteristically exaggerated by their fans) and of United's gradual decline.

There was also a marked difference about the way Liverpool went about their business that stood in deep contrast to the notorious 'white suits' FA Cup Final of 1996. The 'spice boys' were long gone; instead, it was the heavily balding Gary McAllister, who would surely have put any modelling agency out of business had they enlisted his services, who calmly stroked home a penalty to put Liverpool in front following Keane's foul on Murphy.

Owen doubled the lead, capitalising after Silvestre had missed a header and Brown had slipped to leave him through on goal. United's new signing Ruud Van Nistelrooy pulled a goal back in the second half, but there was to be no way back as we fell to a third consecutive defeat against newly buoyant rivals.

United: Barthez, G Neville, Silvestre, Stam, Irwin, Giggs, Beckham, Keane, Scholes, Butt (Yorke), Van Nistelrooy.

Liverpool: Westerveld, Babbel, Riise (Carragher), Hyypia, Henchoz,

Murphy (Berger), Hamann, McAllister, Barmby (Biscan), Heskey, Owen.

Attendance: 70,227

4 November 2001

Liverpool 3 Manchester United 1

Alex Ferguson had announced his intention to do step down as manager in the summer of 2001 and, although he would eventually change his mind, the sense of uncertainty his announcement generated clearly didn't help his club, as he's admitted himself. [2] There were enough warning signs in the events that followed his announcement, you would think, to make United realise they needed to be fully prepared with a coherent succession plan when his departure came for real. You would think.

There was a sense that the team so brilliantly developed by Fergie was splintering into a collection of individuals, one that contained players who were placing their non-football activities over what they did on the field. Dwight Yorke had gone from a smiling, breath of fresh air goal machine to someone whose main headlines were coming via the tabloid press and a sex life apparently far more prolific that his goal count. The David Beckham who had once been shielded from a hostile outside world by Fergie and his United team mates had been transformed by astute image management into a national icon with a media profile that was getting too high for Fergie's liking.

Comments in Jaap Stam's autobiography had suggested simmering animosity behind the scenes at Old Trafford and the player had been quickly sold, moving to Lazio at the end of August, although Fergie was always keen to stress that it was concerns about the player's recovery from injury rather than his criticisms of team mates in his book that had prompted the sale. The manager would go on to declare his decision to offload Stam the biggest mistake of his managerial career. [3]

It wasn't his only mistake that season. The decision to replace Stam with veteran French defender Laurent Blanc – captain of the World Cup winning team only three years earlier – initially looked a shrewd move. However, Blanc would struggle to adapt to English football and was heavily blamed for United's poor early season form that saw them go into this game in fifth place and with worse to come: this loss at Anfield would begin a run of four defeats from five matches in the league. Blanc's French colleague Fabien Barthez was also now looking a far from convincing acquisition while the much-vaunted capture of Juan Sebastian Veron had, whatever the player's unquestioned merits, disrupted the smooth running of what had easily been the best midfield in English football for many years. Veron's cultured, deep-lying passing game was pleasing on the eye, but alien to the high-octane, powerful machine of Keane, Scholes and Butt. It was like putting a Ferrari engine in the best rally car in the world and expecting it to go even faster, when all that happened was an explosion under the bonnet and an ugly mess of parts spread across the road, all of which looked brilliant individually but just didn't work when put together. Veron, despite his many qualities, just wasn't equipped for the rough terrain of the Premiership.

United, in other words, had both sold and bought very badly over the summer and weren't looking anything like a potential Premier League winning side for the first time in years. Indeed, the period in which Houllier was manager was the only period since Dalglish's first stint that Fergie would outspend his Liverpool counterpart both in gross and net terms (with the exception of the brief Hodgson and Rodgers periods). 2001/02 was also the highest spending year of his tenure thus far, yet only Van Nistelrooy would prove to be truly money well spent. Perhaps the signings of Veron and Blanc saw us gambling heavily on our position in English football in order to adapt more effectively to European competition but it wasn't clear that this was working either. Although the Reds had progressed to the second group stage of the Champions League, we'd suffered home and away defeats to group winners Deportivo La Coruna in the process.

Our opponents here, of course, were also in the Champions League for the first time in its modern incarnation. They'd qualified unbeaten from the first group stage, something which hadn't done anything to quell their belief that they were on the verge of a new period of success in both England and Europe. They'd started badly in the Premier League, suffering early defeats to Bolton and Aston Villa, but were unbeaten in six league games since then. Clearly their mood would only be cranked up further by another win against United.

The match illustrated our problems all too vividly. Barthez was busy from the off, dealing comfortably with a succession of Liverpool efforts they were firing off meekly, but finding the room to contrive all too easily. Eventually a better opportunity arrived: Silvestre slipped as Owen eased passed him on his right before the striker curled his shot around the United keeper to give Liverpool a deserved lead. United could do little about their second, a rasping 70mph thunderbolt of a free kick from Riise that Liverpool fans have often proclaimed the best free kick ever scored. It wasn't, but it was admittedly a very good one.

Even United's reply raised questions about whether all was well within the camp. Although it brought us back to 2-1 down and, you would think, into the game, the goal from a shaven-headed David Beckham – who scrappily forced Irwin's excellent cross into the Liverpool net - was only mutely celebrated, certainly in comparison with what you'd expect from a United team in this fixture, and nor did there seem any great urgency to race back to the centre circle in a mission to rescue the game in true United fashion. Perhaps Fergie's rollicking at half-time was still ringing in their ears or perhaps this was a further example of the fragmentation that had resulted from his declared intention to leave spilling onto the pitch.

Whatever the source of the problems, they were certainly in evidence for Liverpool's third goal. Barthez was at fault, coming out needlessly in an attempt to take the ball off the head of Heskey but only taking out Silvestre in the process. The ball fell to Owen, who predictably made no mistake. United carved out further chances in the later stages of the game, but our attacking play continued to look uncharacteristically jaded. This was a fourth consecutive defeat against Liverpool and there was nothing about the performance to suggest the run would be coming to an end any time soon.

Liverpool: Dudek, Riise, Henchoz, Hyypia, Carragher, Murphy, Hamann, Gerrard, Smicer (Berger), Owen (Fowler), Heskey.

United: Barthez, G Neville, Silvestre, Brown, Irwin (O'Shea), Beckham (Scholes), Fortune, Butt, Veron, Solskjaer (Yorke), Van Nistelrooy.

Attendance: 44,361

22 January 2002

Manchester United 0 Liverpool 1

It had been getting better. A run of eight wins over December and January had seen United rise to the top of the league. He hadn't publicised it yet, but Ferguson had decided on Christmas Day to reverse his decision to retire. Many have put United's improving fortunes down to that change of mind, but in truth we'd been playing better anyway, a 5-0 cruise against Derby and a 6-1 crushing of Southampton coming before he'd apparently even worked it out in his own mind.

The problem was, United's improved form would coincide with an even better run of form for Arsenal, who'd lost to Newcastle the week before Christmas but wouldn't lose again for the remainder of the season. Although the Reds would eventually amass a points total close to that which had been enough to win the league in the treble season, the quality of our opponents was far greater than in recent seasons and Arsenal's 87 points would see them win the championship comfortably. To make matters worse, our rivals in this match would sneak ahead of United to finish second – the first time they'd achieved this since 1991 and also the first time in that twenty-one year period that United had finished outside the top two.

United had been five points ahead of Liverpool going into this game but a tight contest of few chances was won by the away side thanks to a Danny Murphy goal. In the second half, Veron had stung the hands of Dudek and Barthez had then made an even better save to deny Riise. It looked to be heading for a goalless draw until, with five minutes remaining, Murphy got in at the near post to collect Gerrard's pass and loop the ball over the United keeper. Giggs came agonisingly close to grabbing an equaliser but he was denied by Dudek, leaving the history books to record that for the second season running Murphy had scored the winner for Liverpool at Old Trafford.

That meant five wins in a row for Liverpool over United and a second season running that they'd completed a league double over the Reds. The defeat would turn out to be only a blip in form for United, who would go on to win nine of the next eleven games. However, Arsenal's impressive form would mean that wasn't enough and a couple of slips at the end of the season would allowed Liverpool to grab that second place.

As the season moved into its final stages, it had seemed there might be the prospect of a dramatic twist that would see the two clubs meeting head to head in a match with higher stakes than ever before. When the Champions League Quarter-Final draw was announced United had been pitted again against Deportivo La Coruna while Liverpool found themselves matched with Bayer Leverkusen. Although the Reds had lost to Deportivo in the first group stage, both ties looked eminently winnable for the English clubs and the draw meant that the winners would meet up in the semi-final. There appeared a real prospect of Manchester United and Liverpool meeting for the first time ever in European competition. Not only that: they'd be competing for a place in the final of the Champions League.

Everyone got very excited. There was even a campaign to get the broadcasters to offer the semi-final as free-to-air in recognition of the scale of interest that would ensue, if it happened, which everyone seemed confident that it would, especially when the two English sides won the first legs. Except the most hyped match between English clubs in a European competition never took place. United did their bit, beating Deportivo over the second leg to cruise through, but Liverpool were knocked out by Leverkusen, shipping four goals in the return leg. Although United fans had relished the prospect of a game against Liverpool in such circumstances, we were inevitably a lot happier with that outcome, especially as Leverkusen frankly looked very beatable opponents indeed. However, a season of disappointments would reach its zenith at the end of April when, with both legs drawn, Leverkusen progressed to the final on the away goals rule. The German club had put out both great rivals and the sense of anti-climax at both clubs was all too evident, but particularly so at United. The Reds ended the season without a trophy for only the third time since 1990.

United: Barthez, G Neville, Silvestre, Blanc, P Neville, Keane, Giggs, Scholes, Beckham (Solskjaer), Veron, Van Nistelrooy.

Liverpool: Dudek, Wright, Riise, Hyypia, Henchoz, Carragher, Hamann, Murphy (Berger), Gerrard, Owen (Anelka), Heskey.

Attendance: 67,599

1 December 2002

Liverpool 1 Manchester United 2

It would have been tempting for most managers, following the disappointments of the previous season, to go for the kind of wholesale turnover of personnel that Liverpool had constantly attempted, with dire results, during the nineties. Had Twitter and Facebook been active back then, you can imagine the level of agitation among supporters anguished at United's relative lack of action in the transfer market. Ferguson, thankfully, was never your typical manager and never one to be swayed by opinion from either the press or the club's own fans, something he'd emphatically demonstrated in that turbulent and crucial summer of 1995.

Instead, Fergie moved to plug a single important gap and, aside from bringing in Ricardo as a reserve keeper, resisted any further plunges into the transfer market that summer. He signed Rio Ferdinand, whose displays during the 2002 World Cup had been outstanding, from Leeds United. It was another capture that had the pleasing double effect of enraging Leeds fans and revitalising United. Not that this revitalisation was evident yet, though. The Reds were in fifth place in the league, having suffered defeats at Leeds and city along with a dreadful home loss to Bolton. Europe was going better, with United finding progress so easy from the first group stage we could even afford a 3-0 defeat to Maccabi Haifa, qualification already having been assured by that point.

Liverpool, meanwhile, had been unbeaten until the middle of November, their form eliciting yet more gurgles of optimism from Anfield as they opened up a four point gap at the top of the league. Their excitement once again proved premature: this first defeat to United since 1999 fell happily within a disastrous period during which the wheels fell off our rivals' pursuit of honours both domestically and within Europe. In the Champions League, Liverpool had apparently shrugged off an early reverse at Valencia and a draw at home to Basel to look well-poised to qualify for the second group stage, following convincing wins both home and away to Spartak Moscow. However, a home defeat to Valencia and another draw at Basel left them out of the competition by the time they hosted United in the league. Not only that, but domestic defeats at Middlesbrough and Fulham and a home draw with Sunderland meant they didn't approach this game in anything like the positive mood that you sense had carried them through recent encounters. And it would get worse. Although we didn't know it at the time, this defeat would form part of an eleven game run without a win in the Premier League, at the end of which any thoughts of the league title returning to Anfield would be in tatters and the main focus of attention was whether their once vaunted manager could hang on to his job.

So it was a good time to be playing them and United wasted no time in settling a few scores left over from recent years. The match will be remembered long into the future among United fans as the one in which Diego Forlan, a much loved player at Old Trafford despite frequently misfiring in front of goal seized his moment and, although possessing a goalscoring record that read only 10 in 63 appearances for the Reds (compare that with averaging more than a goal every two games with his subsequent clubs Villarreal and Atletico Madrid), established himself firmly as a club legend. Not that the performance was as out of the blue as many have subsequently claimed. It may indeed be the case that Diego came from Uruguay and made the scousers cry, but he'd been warming up nicely for the feat with a couple of recent goals against Southampton and Villa. Liverpool found Diego hitting his first, and sadly only, peak at United and he certainly made them remember it.

It made it even more pleasing to witness Liverpool contributing so heavily to their own downfall. The game was a tight affair for the first hour but turned United's way when Dudek failed to deal with a routine header back to him from Carragher, allowing the ball to slip through his legs and gift an opportunity that even Forlan at his most goal-shy would have struggled to mess up. It was the latest of a series of mishaps from Dudek and the United fans gleefully celebrated with chants of 'Jerzy Dudek is a Red'. Despite the number of mediocre keepers coming in and out of Old Trafford in recent years, we could surely rest assured that this would never be the case. The goalkeeper would be less at fault for Forlan and United's second. Although he was beaten at his near post, the Uruguayan's shot after being set free by a pass from Giggs was a scorcher and a fitting way for the much-loved forward to stamp his mark on this fixture for ever.

This wasn't yet a United side in full flow, however, and there were some moments of panic towards the end, especially after Hyypia cut the Reds' lead with nine minutes left. They might have had an equaliser too, had it not been for a stunning save from Barthez to deal with a Hamann thunderbolt. Other than that, their assault on the United goal consisted largely of hopeful balls into the box that the Reds' central defensive partnership of Brown and Silvestre dealt with comfortably or snatched efforts exemplified by a shot from Gerrard that did more to threaten the corner flag than Barthez's goal.

Liverpool: Dudek, Traore (Riise), Hyypia, Henchoz, Carragher, Hamann, Murphy, Gerrard, Smicer (Diouf), Baros (Heskey), Owen.

United: Barthez, G Neville, Silvestre, O'Shea, Brown, Giggs, Fortune (P Neville), Scholes, Forlan (Stewart), Solskjaer, Van Nistelrooy (May).

Attendance: 44.250

2 March 2003

Worthington League Cup Final

Millennium Stadium

Liverpool 2 Manchester United 0

I know it doesn't really make a difference to the result, but it always makes it feel worse when you've spent much of the evening before the match goading Liverpool fans in the pub, confident that their appalling form since the autumn combined with only a single defeat for United in all competitions since December would mean an easy victory for the Reds. Needless to say, it didn't work out that way.

Maybe, since that ultimately crucial fixture congestion caused by the League Cup triumph of 1992, United now approached a final in this completion in an overly cautious manner, seeing it as something to give only passing attention to on the way to much bigger things rather than an important occasion in itself. The performance certainly gave that impression. Liverpool, having seen their own league championship intentions fail to survive the winter, were perhaps understandably more up for it. Although they still had a UEFA Cup quarter-final to come (which they'd lose to Celtic), there was no question this final represented their best chance of not finishing the season empty handed. That said, United had a number of chances to get back in the game in the later stages, only to find an apparently very different Jerzy Dudek in front of the Liverpool goal. The keeper, perhaps keen to make amends for his December howler, had a fine game and played a big part in his side's victory.

It might well have been different had Van Nistelrooy not steered a peach of a cross from Giggs narrowly wide of the upright in the early stages. Liverpool's response was certainly emphatic, a long-range effort from the left from Gerrard benefiting from a deflection off Beckham as it found its way into the top corner.

United went close to getting back into the game when Beckham's long shot was saved by Dudek before Scholes' follow-up was cleared off the line by Henchoz. The Liverpool keeper then saved brilliantly from first Van Nistelrooy and then Scholes in the second half. Four minutes from time, with United throwing everything at their opponents, Liverpool broke from their own half to seal victory via a clinical Michael Owen finish.

In the end, however, perhaps losing the League Cup Final that season was worth it. We certainly put it behind us in some style...

Liverpool: Dudek, Riise, Henchoz, Hyypia, Carragher, Hamann, Murphy, Gerrard, Heskey (Baros) (Smicer), Diouf (Biscan), Owen.

United: Barthez, G Neville, Silvestre, Brown (Solskjaer), Ferdinand, Giggs, Beckham, Veron, Keane, Scholes, Van Nistelrooy.

Attendance: 74,500

5 April 2003

Manchester United 4 Liverpool 0

It's fair to say that, earlier in the season, a United assault on the title had seemed unlikely. Away defeats either side of Christmas at Blackburn and Middlesbrough had appeared to confirm that the Reds, despite a clear improvement on last season, still weren't championship potential and the Reds went into the New Year in 3rd place. That October Arsenal had beaten United's Premier League record unbeaten run of 30 games and looked likely to retain their title. Then, a future United star stepped in, a teenage Wayne Rooney scoring in the last minute of the game to bring victory to Everton and an end to the run. From that point, the champions looked increasingly fragile and, with Liverpool's hopes falling away dramatically, United increasingly grew in strength to emerge as serious challengers. Although it had felt like a significant punch to the guts to any chances of a title challenge at the time, that Boxing Day defeat at Middlesbrough turned out to be the Reds' last defeat of the season.

United went into this game in second place and breathing heavily down Arsenal's necks. The second group stage of the Champions League had been negotiated with ease and, although a Ronaldo-inspired Real Madrid would put an end to European hopes later in the month, the Reds looked as good as at any time since the treble season. Barely a month after their defeat at Wembley, we duly tore Liverpool apart. Van Nistelrooy was looking by some distance the best forward in the league and, when he bore down on the Liverpool goal, Hyypia panicked and brought him down from behind. The Dutchman took the penalty himself and scored: more significantly for the remainder of the game, Hyypia was sent off.

A United side in this kind of form were not going to pass up the opportunity to see off ten men and put the boot into Liverpool in the process, especially as there was a clear possibility that goal difference might be a factor in determining the fate of the title and United still lagged significantly behind Arsenal in that respect. It wasn't until the second half that the Reds increased their lead, however, and the goal once again came from the penalty spot following Biscan's clumsy blocking of Paul Scholes as he entered the area. Once again, Van Nistelrooy tucked away the spot kick emphatically, his ninth goal from nine penalties that season. A statistic that revealed even more about the Dutchman's crucial importance to United at the time was that it was his 70th goal from just 93 games since joining the Reds.

He narrowly failed to make it a hat-trick when he was unable to get on the end of a superb Beckham cross from the right, but Ryan Giggs was following in to make it 3-0. It would prove to be Beckham's last ever appearance in a United-Liverpool game. Following a much-publicised fall out with his manager, Solskjaer had frequently been selected by Ferguson on the right of midfield in the season's later stages and the mercurial product of that great youth team of the early nineties would depart for

Real Madrid at the end of the season. For now, however, the two were on the pitch at the same time and it was Solskjaer's finish through the legs of Traore that made it 4-0 and gave United their biggest victory over Liverpool for fifty years.

It was also United's fiftieth victory over Liverpool in the league but, far more significantly, it maintained an impressive run of form that would see the Reds drop only two further points, away at Arsenal, during the remainder of the season, the Reds eventually winning the league by a five point margin. After a thankfully short period in which United and Liverpool had found themselves roughly neck and neck as also-rans to the Gunners, the Reds had kicked into the kind of run of form that would see them leapfrog both and run out convincing league champions once again.

United: Barthez, G Neville, Silvestre (O'Shea), Brown, Ferdinand, P Neville (Beckham), Giggs, Keane, Scholes (Butt), Van Nistelrooy, Solskjaer.

Liverpool: Dudek, Traore, Riise, Hyypia, Carragher, Gerrard, Hamann, Murphy (Cheyrou), Heskey, Diouf (Smicer), Baros (Biscan).

Attendance: 67,639

9 November 2003

Liverpool 1 Manchester United 2

Roman Abramovich was just one of a number of fabulously wealthy Russians who'd had the fortune to have the right friends at the right time following the collapse of the Soviet Union. At the end of the 2002-03 season, few football fans would have had even a passing interest in who he was or how much money he had. By July that had changed completely. Abramovich had bought Chelsea FC and given them a financial cash injection that made the one Jack Walker administered to Blackburn Rovers a decade earlier look like small change.

With Arsenal flying – they would, remarkably, complete the Premier League season without losing a match – and Chelsea closing in on them, the focus of English football suddenly switched to the capital. For once

United and Liverpool fans were agreed on something: it felt weird, like the whole immediate footballing universe had been thrown out of synch. To give some perspective on why that should be the case, consider a remarkable fact that is all too often overlooked: since the mid-seventies, roughly from when United and Liverpool supporters realised how much they really hated each other, there had only been a single season (1980-81) in which neither of these sides had been closely involved in the pursuit of the league title. This meant that, one way or another, supporters of these clubs under around forty years of age had had a keen interest in the top of the league table for pretty much every year of their lives. They'd either been cheering on their own team in pursuit of the crown or earnestly supporting the main challenger of their rivals.

It's because of this that no other rivalry in English football has been given such a keen edge. Yet suddenly, in season 2003/04, with Liverpool still struggling and United clearly floundering well short of the form that had taken them to the title in the previous season, the entire focus of the league title race shifted away from the two north-west rivals and, for the first time ever, settled on London. For the first in the history of English football, two London clubs finished in the top two positions in the league.

Although United took advantage of Chelsea apparently having more money than they knew what to do with by offloading Veron onto them (he wouldn't fit in there either), the Londoners' summer spending spree would stand in stark contrast to United's worst ever attempt at a transfer-led rebuilding job under Ferguson. During July and August Chelsea spent over £100 million of Abramovich's money to bring in players from abroad of the calibre of Crespo and Geremi, along with talented players from the Premiership like Joe Cole, Scott Parker and Damian Duff. While not all of the signings would work out, it was a kind of throw-shit-at-the-wall-and-see-how-much-of-it-sticks approach to the transfer market that was simply outside the financial range of other English clubs. United, apparently failing to understand that the shit was supposed to hit the wall rather than run out onto the pitch, spent badly, the club entering what Gary Neville would term 'the Djemba-Djemba years' [4]: the eponymous Cameroon midfielder was joined in the United ranks by Brazilian Kleberson, American goalkeeper Tim Howard and French forward David Bellion, a player of considerable pace but one sadly prone to use it to go off in any direction other than the right one.

Although the Reds' capture of Cristiano Ronaldo would mean that the summer wasn't entirely unproductive, the Portuguese winger was at that point still a raw, if very exciting talent and, with the notable departure of David Beckham and evidence early in the season that other joints in the United ranks were beginning to creak, most notably those of Roy Keane, Nicky Butt and an increasingly injury-tormented Ole Gunnar Solskjaer, we needed more immediate answers. To put it mildly, we just didn't have them.

A helpful distraction was at least available in the form of Liverpool's even more hapless efforts. Although their adventures in the transfer market had brought in the promising winger Harry Kewell, the names of their other recruits made United's signings look positively illustrious: Carl Medjani, Anthony Le Tallec and Florent Sinama-Pongolle, anyone? Thought not. Having lost their way half-way through the previous season, Houllier's side continued to splutter and entered this game having won only five of their first eleven league fixtures. United, meanwhile, had managed to get this far into the season with only two defeats, although we sat in third place and were already very much an object in the rear view mirror of Arsenal, four points behind, but set to become a more distant speck in the months ahead.

For now, though, Reds fans could at least bask in the overwhelming shitness of our rivals. United's defence was looking pretty tight at that point and it saw off Liverpool's early pressure to take the Reds into half-time with the game still goalless. In the second half an edginess that had become a distinct feature of the home side's play already that season began to stamp itself on the game. Giggs had almost seized on a huge error from Dudek after the keeper had placed his clearance directly at his feet and, although he scrambled across the goal to make a crucial save, it began a period of play in which Liverpool's defence couldn't get the ball away without it coming straight back at them and ended when a Giggs cross from the right evaded the head of Van Nistelrooy and went directly into the net.

Giggs then grabbed a second, pouncing on a Forlan cross at the far post and seeing his shot deflected into the net by Dudek, who was having another of those days. Liverpool got one back through Kewell, and pressed for the remainder of the game but, though a couple of excellent last-ditch challenges from Ferdinand and Silvestre and woeful finishing from Emile Heskey were needed to bring it about, the Reds left Anfield with all three points for the second season running.

Liverpool: Dudek, Finnan, Traore, Hyypia, Murphy, Biscan, Smicer

(Sinama-Pongolle), Gerrard, Kewell, Diouf (Le Tallec), Heskey.

United: Howard, G Neville, O'Shea, Silvestre, Ferdinand, P Neville, Giggs, Keane, Fortune (Fletcher), Forlan, Van Nistelrooy.

Attendance: 44,159

24 April 2004

Manchester United 0 Liverpool 1

What had increasingly looked a lost season had been rescued three weeks earlier with a magnificent performance from the Reds to defeat Arsenal in the semi-finals of the FA Cup and set up what looked, and would turn out to be, an easy final against Millwall. Even so, a late goal from Porto had seen yet another promising European campaign fizzle out and the Premiership had been out of range for some time, the only question now being whether Arsenal could get through it unbeaten. Admittedly, the Reds' challenge had not been helped by Rio Ferdinand's ban for missing a drugs test in December. We were harshly reminded, if we needed it, of the defender's crucial role in the team since his arrival: those asked to fill in, most notably Mikael Silvestre, did their best but Ferdinand's quality and shrewd tactical awareness were all too conspicuous by their absence.

We'd stutter to the end of the season, winning only a final, meaningless game at Aston Villa in these closing fixtures and, for once, not even a contest against our great rivals could rouse us. This win would help Liverpool to trundle home a place behind United in fourth and secure a Champions League place. It was an achievement that at the time appeared fairly meaningless but ultimately would prove all too significant given the momentous and, from a Reds' point of view, gut-wrenching events to come at the end of the following season, more of which later. It would also, as it would turn out, be Houllier's last game in charge, confirming him as the Liverpool manager with the best head-to-head record against Ferguson's teams.

The game's vital moment came when Gary Neville was judged to have brought down Gerrard in the area and Danny Murphy stepped up to take the kick and, for the third time, score the deciding goal in this fixture.   It turned out to be a far more important goal than anyone, even Liverpool fans, could have imagined at the time.   Had United won this game, it would have left the prospect of Newcastle overtaking them in the last game of the season to secure fourth place and, had that happened, well, United's lack of success in the following season would have been a hell of a lot easier to swallow.

United: Howard, G Neville, Silvestre, O'Shea (Solskjaer), Brown, P Neville (Bellion), Fletcher, Giggs, Keane, Ronaldo, Saha.

Liverpool: Dudek, Finnan (Smicer), Riise, Hyypia, Henchoz, Carragher, Murphy, Gerrard, Hamann, Kewell (Cheyrou), Owen (Heskey).

Attendance: 67,647

Performance record (Ferguson v Houllier)

Games – 15
United wins – 6
Draws – 2
Liverpool wins – 7

Honours

Manchester United – 1 Champions League; 4 Premier Leagues; 2 FA Cups; 1 FA Charity Shield; 1 Intercontinental Cup
Liverpool – 1 FA Cup; 2 League Cups; 1 FA Charity Shield; 1 UEFA Cup; 1 European Super Cup

Transfer Expenditure

Incoming transfers
Manchester United – £182.82 million
Liverpool – £125.4 million

Outgoing transfers

Manchester United – £86.58 million
Liverpool – £59.93 million

Net spend
Manchester United – £96.24 million
Liverpool – £65.47 million

References

1. **www.theguardian.com/football/2013/oct/23/sir-alex-ferguson-mark-bosnich-manchester-united**
2. A Ferguson, Leading, p334
3. ibid, p90
4. G Neville, Red, p 214

5

No Disputing the Facts

Ferguson vs Benitez

20 September 2004

Manchester United 2 Liverpool 1

There had been blips before, of course, but this was the first one since the Premier League began that had the feel of a downward slide. It also felt like we still had some way to go before we got to the bottom. Defeat at Chelsea on the opening day had set the tone for a season in which the Stamford Bridge side, now coached by a Jose Mourinho who'd last been seen running down the touchline as his FC Porto dumped the Reds out of the Champions League, not only won the league by a street but firmly emphasised both how far away from Old Trafford the centre of power in English football now was. United, with a single win in the league thus far, were back in eleventh place and we wouldn't get a glimpse of the top three again until after Christmas. By then it would be far too late to do anything about the destination of the Premier League title.

Although Smith and Heinze had joined at the end of the previous season, the hesitant and faltering rebuilding steps being taken by the Reds during the summer have been emphasised in hindsight by the fact that the two youngsters we recruited at a tender age – Giuseppe Rossi and Gerard Pique – would ultimately go elsewhere in Europe to realise their potential. With transfer windows now an established part of football life, it would take the threat of a move by Newcastle United to prompt the Reds to bid, successfully, for Everton's teenage sensation Wayne Rooney at the close of business, the suggestion being that Ferguson had initially preferred to leave the move until the January window. The acquisition of Rooney would at least provide a much-needed lift for Reds fans, coming as it did after a toothless goalless home draw with his previous club. Along with the acquisition of Ronaldo the previous summer, it was another crucial piece in a rebuilding jigsaw for United that was proceeding slowly, but with some pieces clearly still missing.

Things were shifting at a more dramatic pace at Anfield. Liverpool had sacked Gerard Houllier in the summer and replaced him with Rafa Benitez. Although their transfer business in the close season had been the usual case of overspending on players built up to be something far bigger than they were (the 14½ million splashed out on Cisse being the most notable case of this), Benitez's signing of five of his native Spaniards included Xabi Alonso, who would bring a rare, and thankfully fleeting, touch of culture to their midfield.

They were ahead of United in the league at that point, althoughthe Reds seized the opportunity to begin to put that right here, going ahead after twenty minutes when Silvestre arrived with a late header to put the finishing touch to a Giggs free kick from the right. Pressure from the visitors in the early stages of the second half, however, paid off when Finnan's header across the box struck O'Shea on the leg and trundled over the line for a freakish own goal.

The Reds fought back to re-establish control of the game and it was Silvestre again who popped up with the winner, meaning all three goals in the game had been scored by United defenders. This time it was a Giggs corner that supplied the ammunition and Silvestre again was allowed to hammer his header home unmarked, a beneficiary of the zonal marking strategy on set pieces that would come to be an infamous hallmark of the Benitez reign at Anfield.

United: Carroll, O'Shea, Silvestre, Brown, Ferdinand, Heinze, Keane, Giggs, Scholes (Smith), Ronaldo, Van Nistelrooy.

Liverpool: Dudek, Finnan, Riise, Josemi, Hyypia, Carragher, Alonso, Gerrard (Hamann), Kewell, Garcia, Cisse (Baros).

Attendance: 67,857

15 January 2005

Liverpool 0 Manchester United 1

Hopes still hadn't died of United winning the championship at the time of this game, mainly thanks to an eleven game unbeaten run that had dragged us up to third and would continue to see us progress until well into the spring, when three disappointing defeats late in the season would, for the second season running, see the Reds fail even to finish as runners-up.

A league double over Liverpool always provides some consolation, however. This one came courtesy of Rooney's first ever goal in a United-Liverpool game and was clearly savoured by a life-long Everton supporter who never made any secret of his hatred for his team's city rivals. Rooney ensured the feeling would remain mutual by celebrating the goal, a speculative effort from twenty yards that Dudek allowed to slip under his body, in front of the Kop with hands cupped around his ears.

As was so often the case that season, we made it hard for ourselves, Wes Brown receiving a red card for a second bookable offence in the second half, but a weak Liverpool never looked likely to exploit their numerical advantage and the result was a routine win for the Reds. Even at that stage, it didn't look likely to have any significant bearing on denting the title charge of a rampant Chelsea, but it did have the pleasing effect of suppressing Liverpool's fading hopes of even securing Champions League football the following season, part of a run at the beginning of 2005 of five defeats in eight league games.

Liverpool would go on to be dumped out of the FA Cup by Burnley in the following game and, even though they'd got through the group stages of the Champions League, this had only been on goal difference over the mighty Olympiakos. They would go on to beat Bayer Leverkusen in the first knockout tie, but sandwiched between this was defeat to Chelsea in the League Cup Final, which seemed to put the lid on any chance they had of a trophy that season. United experienced their own disappointment by bowing out of Europe at the hands of Milan, but the strength of the Milanese and other teams in the Champions League seemed to confirm at least that Liverpool were in over their head in the competition and that their removal from the European big boys' playground was only a matter of time.

When they saw off Juventus in the quarter-finals, that did give a mild flutter of concern but they were then drawn to face a rampant Chelsea in the semis, and surely that would bring to an end a run that was as impertinent as it had seemed unlikely. Although United's early departure from European competition had been a huge disappointment, we were at least making progress in the FA Cup, a thumping 4-0 win over Southampton setting up a semi-final with Newcastle that the Reds successful negotiated before Chelsea and Liverpool locked European horns.

It didn't go as anticipated. In a tight two-legged tie, Liverpool saw off Chelsea with a single goal at Anfield. This was worrying. Still, we comforted ourselves, Chelsea would have been the more likely side to go ahead and win the trophy so at least it stopped them adding the Champions League to what was by now a certain triumph in the Premier League. It meant Liverpool fans could toddle over to Istanbul full of hope that would be utterly destroyed by a Milan side who were clearly far better than they were and we could at least end to a frustrating season by enjoying a good laugh at their expense.

The run-up to that final brought huge disappointment for the Reds, losing the FA Cup Final on penalties to Arsenal despite having been easily the better side during the game, but when Liverpool were 3-0 down at half-time in the Champions League Final there was at least a sense that some elements of normal footballing service had been restored.

I'm sure I don't need to run through what happened then and, if I did, I'm sure you wouldn't want to read it so I'll just leave it for both of us to re-run those awful memories in our heads. Chelsea had dominated domestic football, the Champions League trophy was heading to the worst place imaginable and the footballing world, it seemed, had been turned on its head. It surely couldn't get any worse. Could it?

Liverpool: Dudek, Traore, Riise (Sinama-Pongolle), Hyypia, Pellegrino, Carragher, Hamann (Biscan), Gerrard, Garcia, Morientes (Nunez), Baros.

United: Carroll, Silvestre, Brown, P Neville, Heinze, Scholes, Fletcher, Keane, Ronaldo (O'Shea), Rooney (Bellion), Saha (Fortune).

Attendance: 44,183

18 September 2005

Liverpool 0 Manchester United 0

If Alex Ferguson is the remarkable manager I think he is, and his record suggests that he is, he will have understood and even welcomed the kind of ructions that took place in the early part of the 2005-06 season. When things have got into a bit of a rut, good managers know the worst thing you can do is hide from them and hope things sort themselves out. It's like a Shakespearian tragedy: you need a level of conflict that results in at least some of the main figures involved lying dead on the stage.

Of course, representatives of the press and a large number of United's fans, not having his management credentials, saw only a club falling apart. During the autumn and winter, it became a confident assertion of many in those circles that Fergie's biggest mistake had been not walking away when he'd originally intended to do so a few years back. Then, he could have retired with his head held high, his side at the top of the English game as they had been for much of his tenure and with his own reputation as the architect of a footballing dynasty unsullied and unquestioned.

As it was, it was commonly agreed, the Manchester United he'd built was falling apart. Chelsea's riches had seen them overtake the Reds in terms of spending power, their London location also giving them an extra pull in terms of attracting top class players, while Liverpool's unlikely European success a year earlier had suggested a recovery was gathering apace there that would truly make United's life a misery. Not only that, but the takeover by Malcolm Glazer in the summer brought angry protests from United supporters which only deepened when details of the huge loan taken out to finance the deal became known. It was clear straight away that a lot of money previously available for team building would be making its way out of the club in order to pay it off.

Ultimately, all footballing dynasties must come to an end – to believe otherwise is simple foolishness – and there seemed more compelling evidence than ever, both on and off the pitch, that United's period at the top of the game was trundling to a close. Aside from those concerns about the loan, little was known about the Glazers: would they behave with the haste of so many owners from non-football backgrounds and even seek to remove the manager? It cast a further shadow of malaise and uncertainty over a Manchester United team that had enough troubles of its own. Admittedly this goalless draw – the first between the two sides since 1991 – wasn't a bad away point, and took the Reds' unbeaten start to the season to five games. There was, however, a listlessness about this and other performances that would linger well into what turned out to be the most worrying autumn and winter period of Ferguson's reign.

I was amazed, when Tim Howard's autobiography came out in 2015, that so many United fans seized on his comments about fear in the United dressing room as evidence of exactly what the Reds were missing as Louis Van Gaal attempted to rebuild the club following Fergie's retirement. [1] Howard's time at the club was hardly a golden period for the Reds and the finest periods for United were always those when our sides played without a sense of fear. Blinded by nostalgia, many fans seemed to have airbrushed periods like this out of their memories. Fear was evident all over the pitch and it clearly wasn't acting as a positive influence.

A home defeat to Blackburn followed this one and, although the Reds would lose only one league game before Christmas (an embarrassing 4-1 crushing at Middlesbrough), this reverse, along with disappointing home draws against Spurs and city, left United in seventh place in the league. And worse was happening in Europe. In what had looked an easy group, United followed a decent enough draw away at Villareal and win at home to Benfica with a series of insipid performances that brought two further goalless draws and two defeats to leave United bottom of the group and out of the Champions League.

There was a hesitancy about the Reds' play, an uncharacteristic nervousness and uncertainty that left them seriously wanting, particularly against European opponents. An interesting contrast could be made with form in the League Cup where, as usual, squad players were being given the opportunity to shine and were doing so by playing far less inhibited football in a series of displays that brought comfortable progress to the semi-finals of the competition. Perhaps it was the case that, unfettered by the same level of fear and with the League Cup as ever way down the club's list of priorities, the Reds were simply going for it with a freedom and lack of pressure that was noticeably absent from performances in higher profile games.

Liverpool, meanwhile, were in another of those brief periods in which they'd managed to convince themselves, following that unlikely European triumph, that they were on the verge of great things. They'd been busy in the transfer market again, bringing in another Spaniard – goalkeeper Pepe

Reina – alongside midfielder Mohammed Sissoko, Dutch winger Boudewijn Zenden and giant forward Peter Crouch. Despite being European champions, they'd had to qualify from the first qualifying round after a somewhat undignified summer in which they, along with city rivals Everton, had argued like kids about who should be allowed to take part in the competition. Everton had finished in fourth place in the league and precedent suggested that they should lose out as Real Zaragoza had in a similar situation in Spain in 2000. Not only that, but the FA had even released a statement in March the previous year anticipating the scenario and clarifying that this was what would happen should Arsenal or Chelsea win the competition but finish outside the top four. [2]

However, this being Merseyside, it was argued that such a scenario was somehow different (in ways that, apparently, no one outside Liverpool would understand) and a compromise was eventually reached, the FA and UEFA going against all their statements and precedents to allow both to have a shot at qualifying. Everton had, in the event, lost in the final qualifying round amid all sorts of claims about dodgy refereeing and conspiracy theories, suggestions that this was a way of UEFA getting around an awkward situation, yada yada yada. All a bit rich considering they'd had the rules bent to allow them into the competition anyway.

Liverpool's league season had started off with a whimper, with only a single goal from their first four games, three of which, including this one, had ended goalless. It would pick up in the autumn, allowing their expectations of a brighter future again to flourish as they embarked on a run of ten victories in the league and smooth negotiation of the Champions League group stage that would see them in a position from which they could scoff at United's autumn miseries.

Although we didn't know it at the time, this would be the last ever game for Roy Keane in a Manchester United shirt. The legendary captain picked up an injury that forced his withdrawal late in the game. Typically, however, Keane would leave the club pretty much in the manner in which he played the game: noisily, passionately and with a lot of finger-pointing. Indeed, his departure made November 2005 perhaps the most tumultuous and grief-stricken month in the club's recent history, Keane's departure coming just a week before the sad news that an even greater club legend, George Best, had passed away.

Many United fans have taken Keane's side over his fall-out with Alex Ferguson and much of the press did too. Even the normally measured and reflective Daniel Taylor in the Guardian called Fergie's behaviour 'callous' and 'remarkably brutal', even by the manager's standards. [3] Yet it's hard to see how Fergie, or any manager worth his salt, could have handled it differently. The captain had torn into several of his colleagues at the club in a subsequently withdrawn programme on MUTV, questioning their commitment and motivation. True, he was airing grievances shared by many United fans at the time but when a senior player chooses to make his views public in this way it's a clear challenge to the manager's authority, whether intended or not, and he is inevitably forced to take a stance. The choice for Ferguson was really no choice at all: to overlook Keane's comments or take his side (something the manager had never done with any player previously) or remove him from the situation.

Though the latter option was hard for Reds' fans to take at the time, and added to a deepening sense of a downward spiral at the club, it was yet another example of a situation handled decisively and courageously by Ferguson and one that would lead, not for the first time, to an improvement in form. Although many had questioned the manager's judgement, it was a classic Fergie scenario of dramatically turning around a difficult situation to show his support for the bulk of his players and in the process stressing that no one player was bigger than him or Manchester United. And it worked. Though it wasn't obvious at the time, these dark days for Fergie and United turned out not to be portents of apocalyptic gloom, but the passing of storm clouds whose removal would eventually allow the sun to shine on United's fortunes once again.

Liverpool: Reina, Finnan, Riise, Hyyia, Carragher, Warnock (Traore), Gerrard, Alonso, Garcia, Sinama-Pongolle (Sissoko), Crouch (Cisse).

United: Van der Sar, Silvestre, O'Shea, Ferdinand, Richardson, Scholes, Keane (Giggs), Ronaldo (Park), Smith, Van Nistelrooy, Rooney (Fletcher).

Attendance 44, 917

22 January 2006

Manchester United 1 Liverpool 0

If 2005 had been the grimmest twelth months for United fans for many years, a new year was already bringing signs of brighter times ahead. An eleven game unbeaten run in the league had ended with defeat at city the week before this game and, although we'd follow this game with a loss at Blackburn, we'd then embark on a nine-game winning run of a kind we'd not seen for a long time. It was already evident that the Reds' goalkeeping problems had been put to bed, following the acquisition of Edwin Van der Sar from Fulham in the summer, while the capture of South Korean Ji-Sung Park was beginning to look like one of those classic Ferguson low-key purchases of the kind of team grafter who'd always punch well above his weight on the pitch. During the January window, United would make two crucial defensive signings: Nemanja Vidic and Patrice Evra. Notoriously sceptical about the value of mid-season transfers, it was evident that Ferguson had come out of that turbulent autumn understanding that the need to reinforce his troubled squad was paramount. In truth, both struggled initially and their value wouldn't be apparent until the following season. Crucially, however, both would emerge as leaders on the pitch and in the dressing room, making up for the loss of Keane and imbuing the team with qualities that had been in short supply of late.

It was this renewed spirit that chiefly carried United to victory in this game. Both the circumstances and manner of the win made this an encounter to savour for Reds fans. A tight game might have gone in favour of the visitors had Cisse not squandered a golden opportunity on the hour mark, firing over with the goal at his mercy. Instead, an injury-ravaged United held on and grabbed a winner at the death, Ferdinand rising in the area to head home a Giggs free kick. Gary Neville, now captain following Keane's departure, made the moment even more memorable by causing ructions in the away end when he went over to them proudly displaying his badge.

Had United lost, Liverpool would have gone above us into second place; as it was, the win opened up a four point gap and it felt like an important psychological blow too. Liverpool had been the better side for much of the game, but had still not been able to take anything away from Old Trafford despite facing a makeshift midfield missing, among others,

Cristiano Ronaldo, a player now showing signs that his early promise might be leading somewhere very special indeed. It felt like an important turning point for the squad at the time and, in retrospect, that seems even more apparent. United were back.

United: Van der Sar, Neville, Ferdinand, Brown, Evra, Giggs, Fletcher, O'Shea (Saha), Richardson, Rooney, Van Nistelrooy.

Liverpool: Reina, Finnan, Hyypia, Carragher, Riise, Gerrard, Alonso, Sissoko (Kromkamp), Kewell, Crouch (Morientes), Cisse (Sinima-Pongolle).

Attendance: 67, 874

18 February 2006

FA Cup Round Five

Liverpool 1 Manchester United 0

Revenge in the FA Cup was predictably sweet for Liverpool. It was clear both they and United were unlikely to overhaul Chelsea in the league so the stakes were high in this game, with a quarter-final place waiting for the winners and, Chelsea aside, the rest of the last eight hardly looking formidable opposition.

The game, however, took on a more infamous dimension when Alan Smith was stretchered from the field in the closing minutes of the game with what turned out to be a broken leg. Smith was jeered off the field by Liverpool supporters before the ambulance taking him to hospital was attacked by fans throwing missiles and chanting abuse such as 'Munich scum'. Strangely, Smith has subsequently denied that these events took place, [4] although others around at the time have said he couldn't possibly have known as he was under general anaesthetic. Whatever his reasons for doing this (perhaps it was an attempt to defuse any possible future animosity over the incident), it's hard to understand quite why the ambulance men involved (both of whom were Liverpool supporters) would have made it up. Indeed, Merseyside Ambulance Trust submitted a strongly worded complaint to the club following the incident and Liverpool FC even put out a joint statement with United, condemning the behaviour of those involved. [5]

As in the game four weeks earlier, Liverpool had the bulk of the possession and this time made it count, a first half goal from Peter Crouch being enough to take them into the next round and face Birmingham City. They won that game 7-0 and, even worse, overcame Chelsea in the semi-finals before a stoppage time equaliser from Gerrard against West Ham in the final took the game to a penalty shoot out from which they emerged victorious.

By that point United already had some silverware in our own trophy room. It was often commented on by scoffing rivals that, given our somewhat dismissive attitude towards the League Cup for the last decade or so, we certainly seemed happy enough to see off Wigan in the final that season. Relief, I think. It certainly offered a perspective on the way things had dipped for us over the last three years, but in football priorities have a habit of changing with circumstances and, out of Europe and clearly unready to mount a serious challenge for the league that season, we were more than pleased to accept a bit of silverware in a competition that would at other times have been seen as no more than a distraction, and often an unwelcome one.

In any case, that League Cup victory would turn out be significant, signalling both a return to trophy-winning ways, however humbly, and bringing the final moment in a season of upheaval and change at Old Trafford. Ruud Van Nistelrooy, the finest out and out goalscorer to wear the red shirt since Denis Law, was left out of the final, Ferguson favouring the young Giuseppe Rossi instead. At the time it wasn't entirely clear what to make of the decision. Fergie notoriously used the competition to blood and nurture young talent, although the fact that this was the final and the only chance that season of winning a trophy did make the decision a more curious one. The end of the season would bring the answer: Van Nistelrooy was on his way out of the club, sold to Real Madrid.

Could any club or any manager survive the loss of two such players as Roy Keane and Ruud Van Nistelrooy in a single season, Ferguson's critics pondered aloud? They ought to have known better. This was not just any club and not just any manager.

Liverpool: Reina, Finnan, Carragher, Hyypia, Riise, Gerrard, Hamann,

Sissoko, Kewell (Kromkamp), Crouch (Cisse), Morientes (Garcia).

United: Van der Sar, Neville, Vidic, Silvestre (Saha), Brown, Richardson, Fletcher (Smith) (Park), Giggs, Ronaldo, Rooney, Van Nistelrooy.

Attendance: 44.039

22 October 2006

Manchester United 2 Liverpool 0

A single signing in the close season brought the final crucial stage in the evolution of yet another great Manchester United side. As with Cantona, looking for a direct replacement for Roy Keane would have been a waste of time: such a player simply didn't exist. The fact that, in the same close season, Liam Miller – a young man who'd carried the impossible tag of 'the next Roy Keane' when he was bought from Celtic – was shuffled quietly out of the club perhaps offered some kind of low-key acknowledgement of that. United then bought Michael Carrick, a deep-lying passing midfielder and a player whose importance to the team would be severely undervalued by many both inside and outside Old Trafford. Yet he was crucial to this team. Whereas Keane announced himself loudly in games, with ferocious tackles, angry gesticulations at friend and foe alike and thrilling surges up the middle of the field, Carrick dictated play in a measured, calm manner that would have had critics fawning over him had he played in Italy. Here, it was testimony to Carrick's quiet professionalism that he simply got on and did the job, more than happy for others to take the plaudits.

And there were plenty of others in a position to do so, not least Cristiano Ronaldo who, during the previous season had been transforming himself slowly from a raw conspicuous talent into a genuine world class player. By 2007-08 the transformation was complete. In terms of quality, Ronaldo was now untouchable and often unplayable: when he wasn't scoring goals or creating them for others, he was dragging two or three defenders out of the game in order for his teammates to exploit the spaces they left.

Liverpool's purchases in the summer had been frankly under-whelming. They secured the services of the efficient Dirk Kuyt plus Craig Bellamy, that snarling personification of British attacking aggression over guile. Others who came to Anfield in the summer had a familiar ring only to amused observers of the Liverpool transfer merry-go-round: Paletta and El Zhar came, and eventually went, without anyone really understanding why. They would be joined in the forthcoming January window by such figures as Ajdarevic, Brouwer and Duran. No, me neither.

All of which emphasised the return of a once again deeply satisfying chasm between our two clubs both in terms of how effectively they were run and success on the field. Going into this game, the Reds had only lost in the league in a home game to Arsenal and wouldn't suffer defeat again until the middle of December. We'd been at the top of the league since 1 October and would remain there until the end of the season. In Europe, the Reds brushed aside the failures of the previous campaign by assuming such effortless control after the first three games of our Champions League group that we'd be able to experience defeats at Celtic and Copenhagen and still run out group winners.

Liverpool, on the other hand, had already lost three times in the league, including an embarrassing 3-0 thumping by Everton. All of which suggested a gulf of class between us and them that we very much enjoyed seeing demonstrated here. Scholes gave United the lead six minutes before half time after the Liverpool defence had allowed him the kind of space in the area you just couldn't: his shot ballooned off Reina into the air, only for the United man to react quicker than the flat-footed defenders and force the deflected ball over the line.

Ferdinand followed his memorable goal in this fixture the previous year by grabbing the second and making the game safe midway through the second half. This one was not your typical central defender's goal, however. Following early work on the left from Giggs, the ball fell to Ferdinand on the far post and he brought it down to give himself space before crashing his shot into the top corner with a finish every bit as emphatic as his side's victory.

United: Van der Sar, Neville (O'Shea), Vidic, Ferdinand, Evra (Brown), Giggs, Scholes, Fletcher, Carrick, Rooney, Saha.

Liverpool: Reina, Finnan, Riise, Hyypia, Carragher, Gerrard, Gonzalez

(Pennant), Alonso (Crouch), Kuyt, Sissoko, Garcia.

Attendance: 75,828

3 March 2007

Liverpool 0 Manchester United 1

The Reds were flying again. We'd shrugged off the setback of a defeat at Arsenal in January with a run of five straight Premiership wins coming into this game, also progressing smoothly into the fifth round of the FA Cup and winning away at Lille to set up a home return that would see us comfortably into the last eight of the Champions League. Although talk of a treble would prove over-optimistic (the Reds would lose in the FA Cup Final to Chelsea and at the semi-final stage of the Champions League to Milan), the very fact that there *was* such talk showed United were back where we belonged and challenging for honours on all fronts.

Liverpool were making a lot of noise about trophies too. Although they'd been dumped out of both domestic cups by Arsenal, a victory at Barcelona in the away leg of their last sixteen tie in the Champions League had them banging on once again about a repeat of their Istanbul adventures and, following the Barcelona win, people were showing signs of taking them seriously. They'd been on a decent run in the league until recently, too, a run of five wins that had included victory over United's championship rivals Chelsea coming to an end with a goalless draw against Everton and defeat at Newcastle, from which they'd bounced back with a 4-0 crushing of Sheffield United.

In short, they needed shutting up and United did so in the best possible way. As in the home game of the previous season, a United defender grabbed a late winner, John O'Shea this time finding himself in the right place in second half stoppage time to pounce on a loose ball in the area after Reina had parried Ronaldo's free kick. The winner came after Liverpool had spurned most of the game's best chances and with the Reds down to ten men after Paul Scholes had been sent off four minutes from the end.

Although Chelsea would snap at our heels for the remainder of the season, United went on to win the Premiership after a three year gap. Liverpool threatened to spoil the party by once again securing an unlikely looking triumph in Europe. Following victory over Barcelona, they'd seen off PSV Eindhoven before once again facing and beating Chelsea at the semi-final stage, this time on penalties: their win might have set up another potential high profile European game against United, this time in the final, but once again it didn't come off, the Reds having lost to Milan the following evening. Instead, it was Liverpool v Milan again but, this time, Milan thankfully didn't blow their lines and we could celebrate a return to championship-winning days for United while our rivals finished the season empty-handed.

Liverpool: Reina, Finnan, Riise, Agger, Carragher, Alonso, Gerrard, Gonzalez (Aurelio), Kuyt, Sissoko (Crouch), Bellamy (Pennant).

United: Van der Sar, Neville, Vidic, Ferdinand, Evra (Silvestre), Scholes, Giggs, Carrick, Ronaldo, Rooney (O'Shea), Larsson (Saha).

Attendance: 44,403

16 December 2007

Liverpool 0 Manchester United 1

There had been further promising arrivals at United in the summer. Owen Hargreaves joined from Bayern Munich, while the Reds also swooped for a couple of precocious talents in the forms of Nani and Anderson, from Portuguese clubs Sporting and Porto respectively. We couldn't have anticipated then, of course, that Hargreaves would be bedevilled by injuries or that Nani would never quite drag himself out of Ronaldo's considerable shadow, nor that Anderson would keep local pie shops far more busy than he ever kept opposing midfielders. Back then, they all looked pretty shrewd acquisitions for the future. Among the departures was Gabriel Heinze, who'd once looked capable of being United's first choice left back for years before injury had forced him out of the side, allowing Evra to come in and make the position his own. Heinze had apparently wished to join Liverpool but United weren't even considering opening up a can of worms that had remained wisely closed since the mid-sixties and instead agreed to flog him to Real Madrid. Carlos Tevez also arrived on a two-season loan deal.

Despite this activity, there was little sign at the start of the season that 2007-08 might turn out to be the most glorious of all United seasons since the Treble winning campaign of nine years earlier. The Reds had stumbled at the start of the season, failing to win any of our first three games and at one stage sitting in 17th place in the league. We'd recovered well, though, only losing one game since then to move up to second place going into this fixture.

Liverpool, meanwhile, appeared to be slipping back into that familiar position of scrapping away for third or four place in the league, keeping Arsenal company in the Champions League qualification comfort zone while the big boys of United and Chelsea slugged it out for the title. They had, however, made an important signing in the close season, paying £20 million to bring Fernando Torres from Atletico Madrid. He delivered, too, quickly justifying his transfer fee and continuing to build his reputation as a prolific goalscorer. Other signings also suggested Benitez meant business, as he brought in winger Ryan Babel, holding midfielders Javier Mascherano and Lucas and defender Martin Skrtel. As a result of these changes, this was yet another United-Liverpool game that featured a number of fixture debutants, five for Liverpool and a further three in the United team.

Despite these acquisitions, despite being unbeaten in the league until the week before this game and despite Torres scoring almost at a rate of a goal a game, they'd not looked completely convincing. Their early season form had been littered with draws, including dropped points against the likes of Birmingham, Blackburn and Portsmouth, while defeat to Reading going into this game merely seemed to expose frailties within the team that had been rumbling below the surface for some time, as were rumoured rumblings of tension between Benitez and the club's American owners.

United were in a mood to expose them further. Tevez did the damage in the first half, diverting a Rooney shot into the roof of the net from within the six yard area. Rooney might have sealed the victory later in the game when he missed from close range, but the Reds saw the game out anyway, boosting our title chances while for the moment dumping Liverpool outside the top four.

Liverpool: Reina, Arbeloa, Hyypia, Carragher, Riise (Aurelio), Benayoun, Gerrard, Mascherano, Kewell (Babel), Torres, Kuyt (Crouch).

United: Van der Sar, Brown, Ferdinand, Vidic, Evra, Ronaldo, Hargreaves, Anderson (O'Shea), Giggs, Rooney, Tevez (Carrick).

Attendance: 44,459

23 March 2008

Manchester United 3 Liverpool 0

Liverpool had won their last seven games and United had only been defeated once in their last ten in the league, so expectations were high for a close contest at Old Trafford. By now the Reds were involved in a genuine three-team scrap for the Premiership with Arsenal and Chelsea and really needed the three points. A recent unexpected loss to Portsmouth in the FA Cup had put to bed all talk of a second Treble but the Reds still had high hopes for European success and were looking forward to a tie with Roma, who they'd dispatched convincingly the previous year, in the quarter-finals.

We warmed up in spectacular style, overwhelming our opponents with the kind of breathtaking passing at pace that was the hallmark of all great Ferguson sides. An already vulnerable looking Pepe Reina allowed Wes Brown to get above him to head home a Rooney cross for the opener. From there it was one way traffic, and one of those games in which Liverpool, having decided at an early stage that the world was against them, began arguing the toss over every decision going. Mascherano's early challenge on Scholes had already seen him receive a yellow card and yet, despite having already seen Torres booked for dissent, he decided to join in and aim a rant at referee Mike Bennett, who had no option but to give him a second yellow.

Inevitably Liverpool, being Liverpool, were riled by what was an entirely correct and inevitable action from the ref: Mascherano took some time to leave the pitch and, rather than criticise his midfielder's foolishness, Benitez chose instead to blame Bennett, labelling the decision 'unbelievable'.

So we ended with one of those United-Liverpool results where both clubs' fans went home happy: United got to celebrate a win and Liverpool had something to whinge about. Reina was widely criticised for the second goal, beaten in the air by Ronaldo, whose powerful header from a corner doubled the Reds' lead. However, it was Benitez's much-criticised zonal marking that was more worthy of blame: Reina clearly felt he had to come out when he saw that United's most dangerous player hadn't been picked up and by then it was too late. Nani grabbed a third, seizing on a Rooney pass to score from the edge of the area.

From there, the season built to a mighty climax for United. We saw off Arsenal's challenge with a victory at Old Trafford then cruised past Roma in Europe. A defeat at Chelsea was a setback that was instantly shrugged off with a famous victory over Barcelona in the Champions League semi-finals. Again, the possibility of a United-Liverpool Champions League final was quashed when our rivals this time lost the latest of their series of semi-finals against Chelsea. Having secured the league with a couple of routine victories over West Ham and Wigan, the Reds travelled to Moscow for another memorable European final. The events are so firmly embedded in United supporters' brains that they barely need recounting here, John Terry slipping on what should have been the penalty that took the trophy back to London, followed by Van der Sar's save from Anelka that diverted its flight emphatically in the direction of Manchester.

United: Van der Sar, Brown, Vidic, Ferdinand, Evra, Carrick, Scholes, Giggs (Nani), Anderson (Tevez), Ronaldo, Rooney.

Liverpool: Reina, Arbeloa, Skrtel, Aurelio, Carragher, Gerrard, Mascherano, Alonso, Kuyt, Torres (Riise), Babel (Benayoun).

Attendance: 76,000

13 September 2008

Liverpool 2 Manchester United 1

Perhaps the bleating sense of injustice at a referee having the temerity to apply the rules of the game in the last encounter was having an unusually positive impact on Liverpool. They certainly began the 2008-09 season with a sense of purpose that had been absent for years. This victory over United was part of a ten game unbeaten run at the start of the season that saw them establish a position as early leaders in the table.

In contrast, this result and a draw at Chelsea the following week would see United slump briefly to 15th place. Here, we looked very much second best to Liverpool for much of the game, although they needed a late winner to secure Benitez's first league win over United. His side had also had to come from behind to do it, United taking the lead when summer recruit Berbatov set up Tevez in the area to score in the third minute.

United gifted Liverpool an equaliser, confusion between Van der Sar and Brown resulting in the ball cannoning in off the defender's leg for a bizarre own goal. Although a fine save from Reina prevented United regaining the lead in the second half when he turned over a long range effort from Giggs, the home side always looked the more threatening and their persistence gained its reward when Kuyt's cross from the right found Babel in space for the winger to give the home side the lead and, ultimately, the points.

The later stages of the game saw the first instalment in a disciplinary mini-saga in United-Liverpool games for Nemanja Vidic when the Serbian body-checked Alonso to bring a second yellow card and his dismissal.

Liverpool: Reina, Arbeloa, Skrtel, Carragher, Aurelio, Benayoun (Gerrard), Alonso, Mascherano (Hyypia), Riera (Babel), Kuyt, Keane.

United: Van der Sar, Brown, Ferdinand, Vidic, Evra, Rooney, Scholes (Hargreaves), Carrick (Giggs), Anderson (Nani), Tevez, Berbatov.

Attendance: 44,192

14 March 2009

Manchester United 1 Liverpool 4

In its own quaint way, what became known as 'Rafa's Rant' is as deserving of a place in the historical records of managers whose sides threw the league away as was Keegan's famous 'I would love it...love it' explosion in 1996.   At the time it seemed not only strange but completely unnecessary: his team were top of the league at the time and yet Benitez, instead of keeping a square focus on that objective, chose instead to reveal the level of his obsession with their nearest challengers.

In truth, there were probably multiple reasons for his outburst, only some of which were generated directly by the Reds and his opposite number.   Fergie had made some comments about the alleged unkindness of United's fixture list but such observations, whether from Fergie, Wenger, Mourinho or whoever, had become an almost inevitable feature of the league season and Benitez was surely better advised to keep quiet and concentrate on his own situation.   Fergie may well have set the trap – it wouldn't be the first time – but thing about traps is, when you know they're there, they are pretty easy to avoid.   Instead, Liverpool's manager chose to jump in.

That said, like Keegan, his loss of control was probably at least partly generated by his side's first wobbly form of the campaign.   Although they remained top of the league, Liverpool had been involved in a series of disappointing home draws – against Fulham, West Ham and Hull – in the run-up to Christmas.   Remarkably, they would go on to miss out on the league that season despite only losing two games and it was the accumulation of draws like these that would eventually allow United to take a grip on the title race in late January, a position we'd hang onto until the end of the season.   The rant evidently didn't help his side: after a couple of convincing wins over the Christmas period, they slid once again to draws with Stoke, Everton and Wigan to allow United to seize the initiative.

That pre-Christmas form had made previously buoyant Liverpool fans a little nervy, to say the least, and the outburst may also have been inspired by an attempt to achieve solidarity with them.   A manager always makes a mistake when he seeks to curry favour with his own supporters rather than focus on the task in hand.   It was an error Keegan made with Newcastle and one that more formidable managerial opponents like

Mourinho and Wenger have never made. Those managers might, like Fergie, engage in mind games and psychological warfare, but their aim would always be squarely focused on the task in hand and the ultimate aim of giving their side an advantage. Benitez chose as his battleground his supporters' favourite territory of believing the world was against them. I'm sure it had many of his club's fans nodding fervently but, in terms of furthering his club's prospects that season, it was never going to have a positive influence.

The Liverpool boss had even taken the trouble to prepare notes for the speech. This suggested he'd spent some time putting together his research, time that might have been spent doing something rather more constructive. It was impossible to imagine former Liverpool bosses like Paisley or Fagan occupying themselves with such needless distractions: the approach then was keep working at the project and let everybody else do the talking and it had served the club so well during the years when they were a true power in the game. Now they were top of the league again, but Rafa's Rant spoke volumes about the difference between those triumphant Liverpool sides and the club of today.

Everything was in there. He banged on again about Steve Bennett sending off Mascherano last season, bringing in other supposed examples of Bennett's favouritism towards the Reds. Bizarrely, he alleged United were constantly confronting referees, despite claiming that Mascherano had done nothing wrong when he'd done exactly that. I suppose it might be asked how all this was different from Fergie's 'choking back the vomit' remarks all those years ago. But Fergie's was an emotional reaction to something he wasn't happy with and that's something all football managers, and indeed humans in general, are prone to do from time to time. Benitez had gone to the pains of researching, collecting evidence and writing it down before preparing to present it in a formal setting: he'd devoted a serious amount of time dwelling on the issue in what ought to have been the cold light of day.

'I have been watching every single week what has been going on', said Benitez, illustrating the depth of the obsession and the extent to which it had been occupying his thoughts. He unveiled the full, stultifying nature of his club's obsession with United to the world: thinking about the Reds wasn't something you did as a Liverpool fan only when match day came around: you took notes on it and dwelt on it as a permanent part of your life. [6]

Admittedly, while the narrow focus on what United were doing might have cost his side their dominant position in the title race, in a head-to-head situation like this, it paid off. Although United had established a healthy gap between us and our rivals by now, he'd ensured his side were seriously pumped up and apparently chomping at the bit to put one over on us. 14 March 1999 was their opportunity to do it.

As with the season's previous encounter, United took the lead in a game we eventually lost, Ronaldo scoring from the spot after Tevez had been brought down in the area by Reina. Liverpool found themselves back in the game just minutes later after Vidic – with one of few errors in an otherwise fine season for the defender – had been guilty of a schoolboy error when he allowed the ball to bounce and Torres to sneak past him and finish clinically. Just before half-time Gerrard was brought down by Evra in the area and the Liverpool captain put his side ahead from the spot.

Hopes of a turnaround in the second half were already dwindling when Arbeloa put Liverpool further ahead from a free-kick. The foul had been awarded against Vidic, who'd received his marching orders for the second time in as many games against Liverpool for his foul on Gerrard. It only remained for substitute Dossena to complete the embarrassment when he lobbed Van der Sar for a fourth in stoppage time.

Victory for United would have almost certainly put the title beyond reach. As it was, it proved only a temporary blip. Although defeat at Fulham the following week raised some concerns, from there we went on a run of seven straight wins before a draw at home to Arsenal sealed the title with a game to spare. Rafa's Rant may well have had the effect of motivating his side when they played against United, but the long-term result was yet more silverware heading to Old Trafford. To make the title win even more sweet, this was the eighteenth championship for the Reds, equalling Liverpool's record. For the second consecutive season it meant two trophies for United, the League Cup having been secured earlier in the year, although there would be disappointment in the Champions League when we found ourselves outclassed by Barcelona in the final. Meanwhile Liverpool could reflect that their United fixation had brought them a league double over their rivals but, in terms of trophies, fuck all. Their manager had blown what would turn out to be his only real tilt at the league title and put himself in a position from which he'd never really recover.

United: Van der Sar, O'Shea, Ferdinand, Vidic, Evra, Ronaldo, Carrick

(Giggs), Anderson (Scholes), Park (Berbatov), Rooney, Tevez.

Liverpool: Reina, Carragher, Skrtel, Hyypia, Aurelio, Mascherano, Lucas, Kuyt, Gerrard (El Zhar), Riera (Dossena), Torres (Babel).

Attendance: 75,569

25 October 2009

Liverpool 2 Manchester United 0

It felt like we were starting season 2009-10 with ground to make up even before a ball was kicked. Cristiano Ronaldo, now indisputably one of the world's best players, if not the best, had signalled his wish to leave for Real Madrid the summer before but had agreed to stick around another year before now moving on for a fee of £80 million. Having lost a player of such rare talent, United supporters would for years be questioning why the money was not invested, with American owners the Glazer family and the size of their loan payments cast as villains of the piece.

Ferguson himself always denied the claims and it was certainly possible to point to many pre-Glazer instances where the manager himself had displayed a notable frugality and reluctance to spend big when many fans had urged him to do so.

While many United fans waited fruitlessly for that big Ronaldo replacement, instead we brought in Antonio Valencia from Wigan, a solid enough performer but not in the same league (then again, it might be argued, who was?) as his predecessor. It was United's other swoop that garnered more newspaper column inches, however. Former Liverpool starlet Michael Owen had run his contract down at Newcastle, having arrived there after a stint at Real Madrid, and was available for free. All the speculation had been about a return to his former club and some media sources were reporting a 'done deal' to take him back to Liverpool even as United were finalising terms with the player.

Needless to say, the signing caused ructions among Liverpool fans, their nerves still raw from last season's title capitulation. From that point, many even refused to say his name and great amusement could be had when listening to radio phone-ins to hear them simply refer to Owen as 'the other one, him' as they tore into their former hero. The signing was worth it for the entertainment value alone. On the pitch, Owen's injury problems prevented him from having a massive impact, although he will of course always be remembered for a glorious stoppage time winner against city. In terms of pissing off Liverpool fans, however, his value was through the roof. When he came on as a substitute in this game, he became the second player to to play for both teams during the Ferguson era (the other was of course Paul Ince). He'd also be the 100th player used by the United manager in games against Liverpool.

If the loss of Ronaldo was a hugely significant moment for United, then the departure of Xabi Alonso from Liverpool, also to Real Madrid, would arguably have even deeper repercussions for their season and for the future of Benitez. If there was a Liverpool player down the years I'd love to have seen in a United shirt, it was him. Although the club's fans would generally see Gerrard as the man who made their midfield tick, there was no question that the deep-lying influence of Xabi gave them a structure and balance that would be sorely missed as the club now returned to their default mode of limping from crisis to crisis, once again experiencing the customary hangover that followed a season that had promised so much.

They badly needed this win, having lost four times in their opening nine matches in the league. They were also looking down the barrel of a gun in the Champions League, where defeats away at Fiorentina and at home to Lyon left them struggling for qualification. United, meanwhile, were cruising with three wins out of three in Europe: we'd also shrugged off a shock early defeat at newly promoted Burnley to go top of the league after a run of seven unbeaten games.

That run would come to an abrupt halt here, though, as Liverpool displayed a superiority that belied their form going into the game. In the second half, Torres outmuscled Ferdinand to score at the near post before renewing his now semi-legendary tussle with Nemanja Vidic with sadly familiar results: this time the Serbian hauled down the Liverpool forward in the centre circle to bring a third red card in as many games against Liverpool. With United down to ten men but pushing to get back into the game, we inevitably left a few doors open at the back and substitute N'Gog found his way through one of them to finish coolly and secure a much-needed win for his side.

Liverpool: Reina, Agger, Johnson, Aurelio, Carragher, Insua, Mascherano, Lucas, Benayoun (Skrtel), Kuyt, Torres (N'gog).

United: Van der Sar, Vidic, O'Shea, Ferdinand, Evra, Valencia, Carrick, Scholes (Nani), Giggs, Berbatov (Owen), Rooney.

Attendance: 44,188

21 March 2010

Manchester United 2 Liverpool 1

That win against United earlier in the season had only briefly relieved the pressure on Liverpool's manager. His team had failed to qualify for the knockout stages of the Champions League and their league form currently left them floundering outside the qualification positions for the following year's competition. A new year had seen a brief lift in form before they fell to defeats at first Arsenal and then Wigan to leave them once again badly needing a win against their rivals by the time this game came around. As it was, defeat here left them in sixth place, four points short of that crucial fourth position currently held by Tottenham, who had a game in hand.

Benitez was dead man walking. Having brought the club the Champions League and taken them closer to a tilt at the title than any Liverpool manager since Dalglish, there was a feeling that he was losing his grip. His infamous outburst of the previous season appeared to have been the beginning of a consistent sense of the world being against him that, while entirely suited to the surroundings he was in, was not the stuff of a successful manager. There had been long-standing battles between the manager and the club's owners Gillett and Hicks, with reports suggesting that Benitez was unhappy with a lack of support for investment in the transfer market.

To any outside observer the claims seemed laughable. After a costly overhaul of the squad in the early stages of his tenure, Benitez had been given the funds to break the club's transfer record to buy Torres and, during the close season, had been allowed to purchase Alberto Aquilani from Roma, even though the player had been injured for some months and wouldn't appear in the Premier League until November, something that left Liverpool's Xabi-less midfield options seriously short and appeared to have a significant impact on their ill-fated Champions League campaign. Much of the disagreement between Benitez and the owners appeared to emanate from their refusal to allow Benitez to offload Xabi Alonso a season earlier and bring in Gareth Barry, a desire which had looked very odd to those on the outside. Words like 'replacing', 'carthorse' and 'thoroughbred' were thrown around and I'll let you sort them into their correct order. Xabi later hinted that the manager's attempts to offload him the previous year were a factor in his decision to leave the club that summer.

True to form, many Liverpool fans overlooked all of this and, despite their club consistently out-spending United in both gross and net terms during his reign, decided that the owners were at fault and Benitez should have been given even more money to squander. More measured observers among their number, however, blamed the manager for his perceived role in bringing about Xabi's departure, while injuries to Gerrard and Torres during the season only served to emphasise the lack of depth in a squad he'd spent a lot of money assembling.

After this match, Benitez would again draw attention to his alleged lack of resources, pointing to United's ability to include players of the quality of Giggs and Scholes on the bench as evidence of the greater funds his rivals enjoyed, completely overlooking the fact that both these players had been products of the club's youth academy and hadn't cost the Reds a bean. In the event, and despite Liverpool's recent successes in head to head meetings, United didn't have to play especially well to beat their troubled rivals, even after Torres had once again scored, his header giving the visitors the lead in only the fifth minute.

From there it was one way traffic and this time firmly in the Reds' direction. Mascherano brought down Valencia for what was, despite his and Liverpool fans' all too predictable protests, a clear penalty. Future Sky pundits Neville and Carragher were engaged in a furious row in the penalty area as Liverpool players disputed the decision, delaying the spot kick. When it was eventually taken, Rooney had his shot saved by Reina, only for the striker to follow up and score from the rebound. Although Mascherano might well have deserved a red card – it was debatable whether he was the last man or not – Liverpool fans ignored their good fortune in this respect and instead blamed referee Howard Webb for having the nerve to judge it possible for a Liverpool player to foul an opponent in the penalty area.

United's winner was superb. After concerted pressure in the second half, Fletcher's inch perfect cross from the right found the head of Park and the Korean's finish was sublime. Apart from contributing heavily to Liverpool's eventual failure to qualify for the Champions League, the three points were also extremely welcome in a close title race as United went full tilt in an attempt to secure championship number nineteen. However, defeat to Chelsea at Old Trafford followed by a goalless draw at Blackburn a week later meant the Reds fell short of their target by a single point. Having been beaten by Bayern Munich in the quarter-finals of the Champions League and embarrassingly dumped out of the FA Cup at home to Leeds, United had to settle for the League Cup in a season that had earlier promised much more.

Fate also decreed that Chelsea would go to Anfield for a much-win game later that season and to say there wasn't much passion within the ground for a Liverpool win was putting it mildly. 'It's so quiet at Anfield,' sang the Chelsea fans as a poorly timed backpass from Gerrard allowed the away team a lead they never looked like losing. Some United fans saw skullduggery afoot in the Gerrard error but, for me, it was a harsh call to make on the evidence. Not only that, but it wouldn't be Gerrard's last error of that sort, nor his last against Chelsea, and next time he did it he'd prevent his own club from winning the title.

Benitez would, predictably, lose his job at Liverpool in the summer, pocketing a well-publicised six million quid when his contract was terminated. It was remarkable how well liked Benitez remained among Liverpool fans in subsequent years, another example of how their better managers often got short shrift in comparison to those who had overseen such a decline in the club's performances. Houllier had crafted the first Liverpool side to challenge seriously for honours in years; his more cautious approach in the transfer market and measured squad-building had provided most of the groundwork for the side that went on to become European champions. Meanwhile, Benitez hung on to his job, overseeing a clearly stagnating side, constantly complaining that circumstances and finances were conspiring against him, neither of which there was any factual evidence to support: in the process he gave the impression in that last season of simply shrugging his shoulders as his club failed to live up to expectations, as if the situation simply justified his grievances. Yet it was he who, in the coming years, Liverpool fans would be calling for to return to the club to sort out the problems that would, with some inevitability, continue to bedevil them, exactly as they had with Dalglish. But then that particular book, as it would turn out, still had another chapter to run.

United: Van der Sar, Neville, Vidic, Ferdinand, Evra, Carrick, Park (Scholes), Valencia, Fletcher, Nani (Giggs), Rooney.

Liverpool: Reina, Agger, Johnson, Carragher, Insua, Mascherano, Maxi Rodriguez (Babel), Gerrard, Lucas (Benayoun), Kuyt (Aquilani), Torres.

Attendance: 75,216

Performance Record (Ferguson v Benitez)

Games – 13
United wins – 8
Draw – 1
Liverpool wins – 4
United goals – 15
Liverpool goals – 11

Honours

Manchester United – 3 Premier Leagues, 3 League Cups, 3 FA Community Shields; 1 FIFA Club World Cup
Liverpool – 1 UEFA Champions League; 1 FA Cup; 1 European Super Cup; 1 FA Community Shield

Transfer expenditure

Incoming transfers
Manchester United – £198.18 million
Liverpool – £231.15 million

Outgoing transfers
Manchester United – £190.6 million
Liverpool – £161.7 million

Net spend
Manchester United – £7.58 million
Liverpool – £69.45 million

References

1. T. Howard, The Keeper: A Life of Saving Goals and Achieving Them
2. www.theguardian.com/football/2005/may/06/newsstory.liverpool
3. www.theguardian.com/football/2005/nov/19/newsstory.sport3
4. www.mirror.co.uk/sport/football/news/former-man-united-striker-alan-5441799
5. www.theguardian.com/football/2006/feb/23/newsstory.sport1
6. www.theguardian.com/football/2009/jan/09/rafael-benitez-alex-ferguson-outburst

6.

Brief Encounter

Ferguson v Hodgson

19 September 2010

Manchester United 3 Liverpool 2

There is no better feeling for a Manchester United supporter than watching your side stride effortlessly towards the making of history while Liverpool stumble blindly from one crisis to the next. It makes it especially enjoyable when they do so in the misguided belief that they're making progress.

As was so often the case with Ferguson's sides, disappointment from the previous season simply added fuel to determination in the next. Early transfer window captures of promising young defender Chris Smalling from Fulham and Javier 'Chicharito' Hernandez from Mexican club Guadalajara once again revealed a preference for bringing in young, relatively inexpensive talent to be nurtured rather than big name signings. Although again many United fans looked again to the board to dig into their pockets and get us that belated big name replacement for Ronaldo, once again Ferguson would make his strategy work, especially so in the case of Chicharito, who was a revelation. On the other hand, the Reds had shelled out pretty serious cash for a young unproven Portuguese player called Bebe in what would turn out to be probably the strangest transfer of Fergie's reign. Bebe came and tried, largely in the reserves, without ever convincing anyone, apparently, that the move made any sense whatsoever.

There was also a problem with Wayne Rooney. He was stalling on a new contract and the impasse was building to a point where, in the weeks after this fixture, it would become pretty much accepted that he was on his way out of the club. On 20 October, prior to a Champions League game against Bursaspor, Rooney's agent put out a statement from the player to the effect that his desire to leave was due to the club's lack of ambition in the transfer market.

It was a clear attempt to curry favour with United's fans and their rumbling discontent with the Glazer administration. However, at the game that night United's fans made their support for Ferguson clear. We'll never know whether this had any influence on Rooney or not, but eventually, to the astonishment of many, he went on to his mind and sign a new deal. Depending on your viewpoint, this was either a genuine change of heart from the player or a result of his forcing United's hand to make him a better offer. Rooney, having clearly drawn animosity from the United faithful, would have the opportunity to reclaim their support via his performances on the pitch. The can of worms he'd teased open a little further with his comments about the club's ambition would take a lot more to re-seal and indeed rumbled on well beyond Ferguson's retirement.

Still, that paled against the comedy going on at the other end of the East Lancs Road. Roy Hodgson had replaced Benitez as manager and immediately looked a candidate for an early sacking. This wasn't necessarily all Hodgson's fault: he was, after all, replacing a largely popular boss who, despite his popularity, had left him a squad seriously deficient in a number of areas. Hodgson had made an effort to plug the gaps but, whether due to his own poor decisions or the board's reluctance to shell out, the new players had, not for the first time at Anfield, a distinctly average look about them. The names Jonjo Shelvey, Christian Poulsen and Paul Konchesky were hardly likely to set Liverpool supporters' hearts fluttering with anticipation, while Joe Cole, captured on a free from Chelsea, was a player well past his best. It's true that Raul Meireles was brought in from Porto: he went on to be named the fans' player of the year before putting in a transfer request just twelve months after his arrival. Admittedly the sale of Javier Mascherano to Barcelona along with a few other outgoing transfers financed these deals, but once again Liverpool would spend significant amounts while managing to make it look like they'd barely invested at all.

While United got off to an unbeaten run in the league that wouldn't end until February, Liverpool had an atrocious start, winning only one game in their first eight and going out of the League Cup at home to mighty Northampton. This game was part of that early sequence and one of those occasions in which United seemed almost determined to snatch defeat from the jaws of victory, only for Liverpool to prove themselves simply not good enough to seize the opportunity we presented to them.

Initially, the Reds looked in imperious form, deservedly taking the lead through Berbatov's near post header from a corner. It wasn't to be the Bulgarian's last contribution to the proceedings as, in the second half, he received a cross from Nani with his back to goal, teed himself up with his thigh and then crashed an overhead kick into the roof of the net for probably United's best goal against Liverpool in the Ferguson years. A foul from Evans allowed Gerrard to score from the spot and bring the visitors back into the game before a sloppily built defensive wall left enough room for the same player to strike his free kick through it and bring the scores level.

It had the look of a game in which United had done so much to put themselves in a winning position only to let it fall apart and there was a real fear that Liverpool might now do the unthinkable and go on and win it. We needed have worried, however, as it turned out merely to be one of those familiar situations where we made life hard for ourselves before going on to get the job done in dramatic fashion. Berbatov secured the three points when he rose high at the far post to head the goal that brought United the win and made him the first United player for 64 years to score a hat trick against Liverpool. For the record, Stan Pearson had been the last, grabbing three in a 5-0 demolition at Maine Road in 1946.

United: Van der Sar, O'Shea, Evans, Vidic, Evra, Giggs (Macheda), Scholes, Fletcher, Nani (Gibson), Rooney, Berbatov (Anderson).

Liverpool: Reina, Konchesky (Agger), Skrtel, Johnson, Carragher, Raul Meireles (Jovanovic), Maxi Rodriguez (N'gog), Cole, Poulsen, Gerrard, Torres.

Attendance: 75,213

**Ferguson v Hodgson
Transfer expenditure**

Incoming transfers
Manchester United – £27.62 million
Liverpool – £23.85 million

Outgoing transfers
Manchester United – £13.29 million
Liverpool – £26.05 million

Net spend
Manchester United – £14.33 million
Liverpool – -£2.2 million

7

'History Repeats Itself First as Tragedy, Then as Farce', K. Marx

Ferguson v Dalgish, Round Two

9 January 2011

FA Cup Third Round

Manchester United 1 Liverpool 0

The vultures that had been circling for Hodgson were already feasting off his carcass by the time the two sides met again: the club had announced his departure the day before. The 'departure by mutual consent' had followed an embarrassing defeat at the hands of Blackburn and, such was the mood around the club, it was even alleged by some supporters that Steven Gerrard had deliberately missed a penalty during the game in order to accelerate Hodgson's departure.

By now, the club's deeply unpopular owners Hicks and Gillett had also gone, another American John W. Henry taking control and securing popularity with Liverpool fans firstly with the removal of Hodgson, secondly by bringing Kenny Dalglish back into the managerial hot seat and finally with the capture of a big signing in the form of Luiz Suarez from Ajax, a man whose controversial yet brilliant reputation had already gone before him: he'd already bit one player and subsequent events would reveal he had a taste for more. Suarez would play a central role in the next chapter of his club's rivalry with United.

Here, it was business as usual, United securing a routine victory and Liverpool fans whining about it for months to come. Yes, Dmitar Berbatov went over rather easily for the second minute penalty scored by Giggs that proved enough to win the game, but the fact that there had been contact was generally overlooked by our sporting rivals who wished rather to make the point it couldn't possibly have been seen by referee Howard Webb. It was classic Liverpool logic: claiming a decision was unfair even when the ref had got it right. Webb struck himself even more firmly off their Christmas list when he sent off Steven Gerrard in the 32nd minute after a dangerous two-footed challenge on Michael Carrick.

Dalglish predictably labelled the penalty decision a 'joke' while Ryan Babel took his protests online, sharing a photo of Webb in a United shirt after the game, leading to an inevitable sharing frenzy among Liverpool fans. The photo had been culled from a promotional shoot in which several refs had worn shirts from various clubs and Webb had simply been given the United one but, once again, Liverpool fans weren't about to let the facts get in the way of indulging their passion for feeling as pissed off as possible. Not only that, but the narrative around the Dalglish return was that success was inevitable now that he was installed and Gillet and Hicks had gone, so to admit the truth – that the team looked woefully short on quality and it was going to take far more than a change in ownership and the return of an overrated former manager to put it right – clearly didn't wasn't a desirable option for many of them. Being Liverpool fans, a return to the default position that there was nothing wrong with Liverpool so the problem must therefore lie with the rest of the world was adopted. It would be a position they'd keep coming back to during this second period in charge for Dalglish.

United: Kuszczak, Rafael, Evans (Smalling), Ferdinand, Evra, Fletcher (Anderson), Carrick, Nani, Giggs, Chicharito (Owen), Berbatov.

Liverpool: Reina, Kelly, Agger, Skrtel, Aurelio, Raul Meireles (Shelvey), Maxi Rodriguez (Babel), Lucas, Gerrard, Kuyt, Torres (N'gog).

Attendance: 74,727

6 March 2011

Liverpool 3 Manchester United 1

With United poised to win a nineteenth championship that would finally see them overtake Liverpool in the record books, a Liverpool side apparently rejuvenated under Dalglish clearly saw it as crucial to inflict a defeat on the Reds and preserve the slim chance of it not happening. United had been unbeaten in the league until a surprising 2-1 defeat at Wolves in February had suddenly interrupted what had looked like smooth progress to the title. Defeats at Chelsea and in this game meant three reverses in four games on the road and suddenly our position at the top of the Premier League appeared far less secure.

After losing to Blackpool in Dalglish's first league game, his side had then embarked on a steady run before coming down to earth with a defeat at West Ham the week before this fixture. Signs that they were still reassuringly prone to make bad decisions and knee jerk responses in the transfer market remained evident, however. They'd wailed and howled in time-honoured fashion when Fernando Torres had left them for Chelsea at the end of the transfer window, then responded by spending a British record fee on his replacement Andy Carroll from Newcastle, a forward heavy on nuisance value but short on skill who nevertheless had received the typical Anfield welcome as a conquering hero.

There had then come a rare period of mutual joy among United and Liverpool fans when a constantly misfiring Torres looked anything like value for the money lavished to take him to Stamford Bridge. Although they'd spend the cash they got from his sale hastily and unwisely, the sale itself was actually good business for Dalglish, Torres having looked very much less like his old self since the summer. Following the move, this initially put down to a suspicion that he'd been wanting out but, in time, it began to look a simply a case of his no longer being the player he once was.

Anyway, none of this detracted from the prevailing view among Liverpool fans that, with 'King Kenny' back at the helm, the club would soon be contenders again whatever happened in the transfer market. Hardly shrinking violets when it came to exaggerated displays of emotion, the Anfield crowd had vociferously proclaimed his return to Europe in the rather understated setting of a home Europa Cup tie against Sparta Prague that they'd scraped through with a single goal, before the side's position in European football was properly exemplified by a lacklustre display and defeat to Sporting Braga in the next round. There seemed to be a strange belief among Liverpool supporters that Dalglish had a track record in European football management, when actually his pedigree amounted to a single dismal campaign in charge of Blackburn Rovers. Not for the first time, Liverpool fans had been forced to reinvent history in their attempts to convince themselves better things were on the horizon. The second coming of this particular messiah having duly arrived, the first one clearly had to be suitably embellished to include things that never actually happened.

Inevitably the same level of hysteria accompanied this victory, in one of those games in which it seemed a combination of self-generated hyperbole at Anfield and a lack-lustre United were enough to give Liverpool the edge. Although Berbatov had come close to giving the Reds the lead when he hit the post early on, a ragged-looking United defence (missing both Ferdinand and Vidic) then allowed Suarez to tear into the area and set up Kuyt for a tap in. It was a lead Liverpool never looked like squandering and it was doubled when Kuyt rose to head a second.

Liverpool were lucky to have eleven on the field when Carragher wasn't sent off after a dreadful challenge on Nani that saw the Portuguese winger forced out of the game. Whether it was this that led to a similarly rash tackle by Rafael soon afterwards or not, the Brazilian full back also didn't receive his marching orders despite the customary mass hysterical reaction from the Liverpool players and crowd, who displayed their usual tendency to react to a bad tackle as if it were a mass killing spree. In truth, both players probably deserved to be sent off.

United went three down in the second half when Suarez's free kick was saved by Van der Sar only for Kuyt to follow up and complete his hat trick. It was the first hat trick for a Liverpool player against United since Beardsley's classy performance 21 years earlier, a fact that did nothing to dispel the 'second coming' mania afflicting Anfield at the time. Although Chicharito pulled a goal back for the Reds in stoppage time, it was inevitably far too late: in truth, United had looked unlikely to get anything from the game ever since Kuyt had opened the scoring.

Defeat against Liverpool always rankled, of course, especially so as this one was followed by the normal exaggerated nonsense from the Anfield faithful about world domination being just around the corner. In the event, it turned out there had been nothing to worry about. It was another false dawn for Liverpool while the Reds suffered only one further defeat – away to Arsenal – in the remainder of the season and went on to win the Premier League by nine points. This nineteenth championship emphasised the astonishing turnaround in British football that Alex Ferguson had engineered. Since 1990 Liverpool had rarely even threatened to add to their total, while Fergie had brought a remarkable twelve Premier League trophies to Old Trafford to make Manchester United now officially the most successful side in English football history. On reflection, it was good that Dalglish had been there to see it.

Liverpool: Reina, Johnson, Aurelio (Kyrgiakos), Carragher, Skrtel, Raul Meireles (Carroll), Gerrard, Maxi Rodriguez, Lucas, Suarez (Cole), Kuyt.

United: Van der Sar, Evra, Brown, Smalling, Rafael (O'Shea), Giggs, Carrick, Nani (Chicharito), Scholes (Fletcher), Berbatov, Rooney.

Attendance: 44,753

15 October 2011

Liverpool 1 Manchester United 1

If the arrival of Abramovich at Chelsea began a change that had affected the whole power structure of the Premier League, the takeover of Manchester city by an oil-rich sheikh took it to another level. Long consigned to the status of mere irritating small-time locals in a rivalry that had come a long-distant second (or, when Leeds had been around, third) in importance to Reds supporters, the enormous influx of money into city had made them serious contenders pretty much overnight. Last season they'd knocked United out of the FA Cup at the semi-finals stage, scuppering any thoughts of another double, and finished third in the league. They were now in the Champions League and already, it was clear, looking a good bet for their first Premier League title.

If there were any thoughts that this might lead to city replacing a still ailing Liverpool outfit as the priority rivals for United, they would be put to bed for good by this match, which saw tension between the the two clubs reach still greater heights while offering a stark example of the very different value systems at work within the clubs. These had always, rather than the mere accident of geography, provided the basis for the mutual hostility that existed between United and Liverpool, so pronounced that the events that took place here even managed to eclipse the 6-1 hammering United would suffer at the hands of city a week later.

There had been changes at United in the summer. The departure of Edwin Van der Sar in particular had caused concern among those who recalled how badly we'd struggled to replace Peter Schmeichel. We'd signed David De Gea as a replacement and, although he would go on to establish himself as one of the club's great keepers, at this point he was struggling. Paul Scholes had also retired, at least for now: at his testimonial in the summer, Scholes had characteristically seemed more inclined simply to walk off at the end and avoid a lot of fuss, only deigning to complete a lap of honour when accompanied by a bunch of his fellow youth team graduates. Veteran defenders John O'Shea and Wes Brown had also left the club. Young defender Phil Jones had arrived from Blackburn and the signing of winger Ashley Young from Aston Villa had bolstered wide options.

Liverpool fans, meanwhile, had been getting excited on social media about 'the last time' Dalglish had been given money to spend. They seemed to think this had brought Barnes and Beardsley to the club when, in fact, his last spending spree had seen the likes of David Speedie and Jimmy Carter arrive and announced the beginning of Liverpool's decline. When handed the cheque book, he duly picked up where he'd left off, spending over £50 million on Jordan Henderson, Charlie Adam, Stewart Downing, Jose Enrique and Sebastian Coates. While Liverpool fans continued to display trust in their manager's managerial prowess even in the wake of that Andy Carroll purchase, all anyone else could see was a bunch of signings of mediocrities and, in Coates' case, speculative punts on unproven talent. And so it would prove, with only Henderson and the injury-troubled Enrique having any kind of future at the club.

United went into this game unbeaten in the league, while the optimism that had prevailed through the summer at Liverpool had by now begun to evaporate as Premiership reality set in. A draw against Sunderland at home in the first game had been followed by defeats at Stoke and Spurs, the latter a 4-0 hammering. Here, the sharing of the points with United would prove almost incidental to other events that took place on the pitch and after the match.

By then the talking points would have little to do with the two goals:

Gerrard had opened the scoring for Liverpool with a second half free kick before substitute Chicharitio rescued a point for the Reds with a header nine minutes from the end. Early reports on the contest understandably showed a lack of awareness of anything else that had gone on, the BBC Sport website simply recording 'a prolonged bout of bickering' between Evra and Suarez. After the game, however, Evra made a formal complaint alleging he'd been the victim of racial abuse from the Liverpool player.

I can't speak for all United fans on this, but I've often pondered how I'd have reacted had the boot been on the other foot and I'm absolutely clear on this point: I'd certainly have found it impossible to take the side of the player concerned unless it was absolutely clear he was innocent of the charges. There was a precedent of sorts. Ian Wright had once alleged he'd been racially abused by Peter Schmeichel in a United-Arsenal game. Unfortunately Wright had chosen to say nothing at the time of the game and made his allegations in the press rather than submit an official complaint, which meant no formal investigation could take place. I wasn't willing to condemn Schmeichel on the basis of an unproven allegation, but it was disappointing we hadn't been able to establish what had gone on and, had the keeper proved to be guilty, I'd have struck him off my list of United heroes long before he ever turned out in a city kit.

I can't say that there weren't Liverpool fans that felt the same way about Suarez. Indeed, I'm sure there were. The general mood among them, however, showed a determination to throw their support behind their own player. This was despite Suarez admitting to using the word 'negrito' to address Evra during the game: the term itself is at best highly patronising and clearly carries racist connotations, yet suddenly a whole torrent of Liverpool supporters proclaiming a specialist understanding of the Spanish language and Uruguayan dialect argued that it was nothing of the sort. You'd have thought that, even allowing for this view, they might have understood why Evra had been unhappy. Not a bit of it: in a contortion of logic peculiar, it seems, to Liverpool supporters, he's frequently been branded a liar over the issue, despite the fact that at no point was it ever suggested, even by Suarez, that he'd made the incident up.

Even worse, Dalglish came out unequivocally to back his player, even to the extent of sending his players out for training wearing t-shirts proclaiming their support for Suarez The rest of the footballing world, and indeed the majority of the country, looked on with a mix of disbelief and outrage. Some former players came out to condemn the action as a setback for football's anti-racism campaigns [1] while city manager Roberto Mancini was among others who came out to denounce the gesture. [2]

When Suarez received an eight-game ban Suarez following the investigation, the national press were pretty much united in their opinion that the decision and level of punishment were appropriate. [3] The Liverpool Echo was left as a loan voice in support of Suarez. Comments from the paper's James Pearce were particularly telling. He pointed out that no United players had made statements in support of Evra, a claim that appears to labour under the mistaken belief that Evra was had something to prove in the case when, in fact, the central issue that needed to be decided upon was whether the language used constituted racial abuse, something that was clearly best determined by a linguistic expert rather than any of United's Spanish-speaking players. [4]

It's difficult not to conclude that, had the club distanced itself more firmly from Suarez's actions, they'd have come out of the scenario with something of their cherished (if always bogus) squeaky clean image salvaged. A simple no comment on the basis that the investigation had not yet taken place would surely have sufficed alongside an assurance that the club took seriously all such accusations and would cooperate with the inquiry. And it would have been easy to prevent the T-shirts incident: even if we're to give Dalglish and his players the benefit of the doubt that they'd just overlooked the wider connotations of their actions in their determination to support a colleague, the club should have been aware of the dangerous and irresponsible message it sent out and someone senior at the club could surely have put a stop to it.

Bizarrely, many Liverpool fans went online to draw comparisons with the Cantona kung fu incident and United's subsequent support for the player. However, United had suspended Cantona before the FA took action and there had never been any suggestion from within the club that he'd done nothing wrong. Imagine the furure had United players gone out wearing Cantona T-shirts following the incident. And imagine Fergie ever allowing them to do so.

There was no suggestion of Liverpool taking a similar initiative and banning Suarez, even though the player had admitted to using the language that had caused offence. Of course United's fans had continued to love Cantona after the incident, but there had never been any attempt to portray him as squeaky clean. Nor, indeed, had there been any kind of racist angle to his behaviour: indeed, he'd clearly been on the receiving

and Liverpool were clearly set up to exploit this. When Andy Carroll's huge frame was used to block and distract De Gea on a corner, Daniel Agger was allowed a free header that gave the home side the lead.

It was a disappointing setback for the Reds, who were the better side throughout the game, but we got back on level terms when Rafael crossed for Park Ji-Sung to rifle his shot past Reina. United had further chances to score but failed to capitalise on them against a vulnerable looking Liverpool defence and paid the price in the closing minutes, Kuyt exploiting space on the left of what should have been the United defence to beat De Gea at his near post. Kuyt missed an opportunity to extend his side's lead in the closing seconds but the crucial damage had already been done.

Liverpool: Reina, Jose Enrique, Agger, Carragher (Kuyt), Kelly, Skrtel, Gerrard (Bellamy), Maxi Rodrigues (Adam), Henderson, Downing, Carroll.

United: De Gea, Evra, Evans, Smalling, Rafael, Giggs (Berbatov), Park, Carrick, Scholes (Chicharito), Valencia, Welbeck.

Attendance: 43,592

11 February 2012

Manchester United 2 Liverpool 1

Liverpool's legendary obsession with keeping all issues behind closed doors had inevitably proved difficult to maintain in the modern era. During the seventies and eighties a careful control had prevailed regarding what messages would be shared with the outside world. Secrecy was maintained with the efficiency of a war-time operation and talking points for the outside world to chew over kept to a well-managed minimum. Now, in a world of wall-to-wall media coverage and fans' forums, such an approach was impossible.

Other changes to the game played a part in revealing to the world what some would have preferred to keep well hidden. Multiple cameras at football grounds, for example. On-field incidents could be captured from every angle so that, for the offender, there really was no hiding place. The same went, of course, for those who sought to protect that offender: getting it wrong meant you could look very silly very quickly. And if you went a stage further and denied that an incident had even taken place, your ascension up the scale of foolishness would be a very fast one indeed.

It was inevitable that the focus would be on Evra and Suarez coming together on the same pitch for the first time since the infamous encounter in October; inevitable, too, that the cameras would be focusing on the customary pre-match handshake. So when Evra put his hand out to receive that of Suarez, only for the Uruguayan to ignore it and move on, there was no question of the interaction, or lack of it, going unnoticed. Not only that, but the failure to receive the handshake went against what his manager had assured the world would happen, Dalglish having stated very clearly in the build-up to the game that the intention was for a line to be drawn under the incident.

In his post-match interview, Dalglish appeared to contend that a handshake had actually taken place. To be charitable, presumably the basis for that was a misplaced expectation that his player wouldn't let him down, although it was difficult to imagine that there hadn't been some awareness in the Liverpool camp of the kerfuffle that took place among the players following the incident. The manager's comments certainly didn't help to quell the rising momentum of support for Suarez among Liverpool fans on social media who sought to claim, against all evidence, including surely their own eyes, that it was Evra who had refused the handshake. Even for Liverpool fans, seasoned experts at defending the indefensible, this was a bit special.

In a very good Guardian Sportblog article following the game, Daniel Taylor lamented Liverpool's 'paranoia', criticizing the club for an endemic tendency to be 'outraged over everything and ashamed of nothing. [6] If anyone thought the club had already plumbed the depths over the Suarez affair, their response to this new incident showed that they really didn't understand how low the club really could go.

Thankfully, someone at Liverpool FC finally showed some sense over a matter that was now dragging the club's name even further into the gutter. Managing Director Ian Ayre released a strong statement criticising Suarez. It was the first public criticism of the striker, some four months after the original incident had taken place and you can only conclude that, had such a statement been released at the time of the original offence,

Liverpool FC might have saved themselves a hell of a lot of reputational damage. Dalglish then came out and apologised for what he'd said in his post-match interview. This in turn provoked an apology from Suarez on the club's website, where he stated clearly that he ought to have shaken hands.

It's only possible to speculate how much longer the matter might have rumbled on had someone in the club's hierarchy not finally taken belated action to bring the matter to a close. It was certainly difficult to see Suarez taking the initiative. Three months later he was still insisting he'd done nothing to warrant the original ban and that the FA had acted simply because 'they had to get rid of a Liverpool player'. [7] Given that remark, it's hardly surprising that Suarez remains such an icon among the club's fans, although the FA should have wished to go to such lengths to victimize a mid-table club wasn't explained.

Bad feelings following the handshake (or rather lack of one) rumbled beneath the surface and threatened at times to spill over into the game itself. Towards the end of a goalless first half, a clearly riled Suarez kicked the ball at force into the crowd. Evra's immaculate handling of the booing from a hostile crowd at Anfield wasn't being matched by Suarez in dealing with the chants directed at him at Old Trafford, and there were angry scenes in the tunnel as the two sides went off at half-time.

After the interval, it was United who kept their composure to establish a two goal lead. A minute after the break Liverpool's defence failed to deal with a corner and Rooney, finding himself unmarked at the far post, pounced to fire home. Three minutes later the same player was set free in the area by Antonio Valencia to double the lead.

It was, inevitably, Suarez who got the goal that brought Liverpool back into the game ten minutes for time, reacting quickest when Rio Ferdinand failed to deal convincingly with a free kick into the United box. But it wasn't enough. United celebrated a win that kept our hopes of a twentieth title very much alive. Evra received heavy criticism for excessively celebrating in front of the Stretford End, although it just seemed to me that this was a perfectly understandable release of emotion from a player who had received a hell of a lot of abuse over the last four months purely for standing up for his human rights. The dignity he'd displayed during that period had rarely received comment and, for me, it was entirely reasonable that eventually a need to blow off steam would surface.

While Liverpool laboured among the also rans, at this point there remained a close title race for United to contend with and, in case, you were living in Antarctica at the time, I'd better explain that we blew an eight point lead going into the final games and then city came from a goal down in stoppage time in the last game to win the title. I suppose you may have missed it because it doesn't get shown on the telly very often.

United: De Gea, Evra, Ferdinand, Evans, Rafael, Giggs, Carrick, Scholes, Valencia, Rooney, Welbeck.

Liverpool: Reina, Johnson, Jose Enrique, Agger, Skrtel, Gerrard, Henderson, Kuyt (Adam), Downing (Bellamy), Spearing (Carroll), Suarez.

Attendance: 74,844

Performance Record

(Ferguson v Dalglish, Round Two)

Games – 5
United wins – 2
Draws – 1
Liverpool wins – 2
United goals – 6
Liverpool goals - 7

Honours

Manchester United – 1 Premier League; 1 FA Community Shield
Liverpool – 1 League Cup

Transfer expenditure

Incoming Transfers
Manchester United – 101.4 million
Liverpool – £111.28 million

Outgoing Transfers
Manchester United – £42.65 million
Liverpool – £79.1 million

Net spend
Manchester United – £58.75 million
Liverpool – £32.18 million

References

1.   www.theguardian.com/football/2011/dec/22/liverpool-shirts-luis-suarez)
2.   www.telegraph.co.uk/sport/football/teams/manchester-city/9006169/Manchester-City-manager-Roberto-Mancini-believes-Liverpools-T-shirt-support-of-Luis-Suarez-was-a-mistake.html
3.   www.theguardian.com/football/blog/2011/dec/21/luis-suarez-liverpool-racism-fight
4. ibid
5. www.bbc.co.uk/sport/0/football/16776011
6.   www.theguardian.com/football/blog/2012/feb/11/liverpool-kenny-dalglish-luis-suarez
7. www.mirror.co.uk/sport/football/news/liverpool-striker-luis-suarez-still-847934

8

Going Out at the Top

Ferguson v Rodgers

23 September 2012

Liverpool 1 Manchester United 2

When United returned to Anfield for what turned out to be Fergie's final visit as manager, Dalglish was no longer there. Despite the near-euphoria that had accompanied the return of 'King Kenny', their season had spluttered to the kind of ignominious close that was such a familiar scenario for the club in recent times. They had, it was true, won the League Cup and only lost to Chelsea in the FA Cup Final, but their league form was dismal. A mere five Premier League wins since the New Year saw the club cast far adrift from the Champions League places. An eventual eighth place, tied on points with Fulham, represented a hugely disappointing return, especially given the sums the manager had been allowed to splash out.

Even so, after Brendan Rodgers took the helm in the summer to begin an initially promising spell, there would be many among the Liverpool support who would respond to every bad result with a claim that this would never have happened under 'King Kenny'. Realism and logic remained concepts alien to so many among that body of people. It was true that the new manager had got off to a bad start in the league – his team were without a win going into this game and still without one coming out of it – but he'd clearly already made steps to stem and reverse the decline that had set in, moving the likes of Bellamy and Adam out of the club and packing Andy Carroll off on loan, while spending shrewdly to bring in the underrated Daniel Sturridge and the promising Philippe Coutinho. Both would prove highly successful signings.

He'd also already shown signs that he was equipped to deal what had become known as 'the Suarez situation', a term now synonymous with Dalgish's second stint in charge. The game and its coverage in the media had changed massively since his predecessor had previously been at the helm at Anfield and the need to manage the club as it related to the outside world as well as internally was now a far more pronounced aspect of the job role. Although the season would eventually end with Suarez biting somebody, there was no doubt Rodgers had some success in getting the player to focus more on his game and his professional conduct within it and this would reap rewards, Suarez going on to bag 30 goals over the season. He and the club also prepared shrewdly for his inevitable departure, keeping him at the club the following summer and getting him to sign a new contract before he was eventually allowed to move to Barcelona.

United, meanwhile, made the summer's most crucial signing. Robin Van Persie declared himself fed up with the seasonal embarrassment of celebrating third or fourth place in an Arsenal side that'd for a long time looked unable to aspire to anything higher, and wanted out. The oil millions of Manchester city appeared initially to put them in pole position to secure his signature but RVP had ignored their advances and opted instead for a move to United. History will record that we only really got one good season out of him, but what a season it was. His influence was already apparent. Despite a loss at Everton on the opening day, we'd certainly looked like we meant business in the games after that, scoring ten goals in three games, including a Van Persie hat-trick at Southampton.

During the week prior to this game an independent panel had, after many years, revealed details of what had caused the Hillsborough disaster and subsequent cover-up. Although there are some among the United support who've chosen to add references to the disaster to their arsenal of 'banter', I think, and hope, they are very few. It's more common for me to meet fellow Reds who express sympathy for the victims, though there are a disappointing number who will add to that 'they should have let it go by now, though'. I couldn't disagree more. Indeed, I'd go so far as to say that the campaign for justice over Hillsborough is the one thing to have come out of Liverpool Football Club for which I have unreserved respect.

If you know your history as a United fan, it really shouldn't be otherwise. It scarcely needs to be said that we, more than any other club in English football, have experienced significant tragedy and loss during our history. Not only that, but Manchester United emerged from the working class communities of Manchester: United is an institution borne of the working class solidarity that spawned and nurtured movements like the chartists and other campaigns for the rights of working class people. All of this has its history in the assembly at St Peters Fields that resulted in the Peterloo massacre of 1819, where a crowd of 60,000 peaceful protestors were attacked by a cavalry charge that killed fifteen and wounded hundreds more.

For decades the authorities sought to portray Peterloo as the unintended result of the army having to go in and sort out a situation that was getting out of control. There was a government crackdown on the Manchester Observer, a paper who'd helped organise the protest, and its owner James Wroe was imprisoned for twelve months, while other charges against his family were only dropped on condition that the 'libel' being spread by the paper in the wake of the massacre ceased. The courts then imprisoned five of the gathering's organisers and acquitted all those among the calvary against whom a civic action had been brought, ruling that their actions had been justified to disperse an unruly gathering. The Home Secretary conveyed to them the thanks of the Prince Regent for their efforts in keeping the peace.

It wasn't for many years that the truth about Peterloo was admitted or even allowed to be spoken about openly and it was only due to the tenacity of the victims' families and supporters that the truth eventually came to light. [1] The campaign over the Hillsborough disaster was borne of the same spirit. That's why I've got no time for any United fan who criticises their actions. Nor have I, incidentally, for those many Liverpool fans in recent years who've sought to use Hillsborough against me when I've made any sort of criticism of their club: the victims of Hillsborough deserve far more than to have their memories abused in such a way. Ditto the attempt to claim that the chant 'Always the victims – it's never your fault' somehow refers to Hillsborough when it clearly surfaced at the time of the Suarez incident, something which any genuine Liverpool supporter must know. Hillsborough was a terrible tragedy: it should not be disrespected by fans of other clubs and nor should it be used as a rhetorical weapon by Liverpool supporters.

Anyway, it was understandably the case that Liverpool would wish to commemorate the report's findings and it so happened that the next game was this one. With nerves still raw over the Suarez issue, there was predictably some concern that tensions would surface at the most inappropriate time. As it was, Suarez shook hands with Evra while Bobby Charlton presented flowers to Ian Rush and, together, Ryan Giggs and Steven Gerrard released 96 red balloons into the skies over Anfield. The United fans present behaved themselves impeccably although, if Liverpool supporters thought we were going to stay silent while they sang 'You'll Never Walk Alone', they were sorely mistaken. It was at that the point that the harmony ended and battle commenced, which is entirely as it should be.

On the field, United were pretty terrible, the sending off of Jonjo Shelvey in the first half giving us a numerical advantage we completely failed to use to make use of, and we went behind to a Gerrard volley early in the second half. Minutes later United were level thanks to a superb left-footed effort from Rafael. Nine minutes from the end Johnson fouled Valencia and Van Persie made no mistake from the penalty spot to give the Reds an important, if unconvincing, victory.

Brendan Rodgers continued his initiation into the role of Liverpool manager by blaming the defeat on the referee, arguing that Mark Halsey had been wrong to apply the rules of the game and send off Shelvey while claiming he didn't know why Valencia had gone down for the penalty, when everyone else could see it was because he'd been tripped. [2]

Liverpool: Reina, Johnson, Agger (Carragher), Kelly, Skrtel, Gerrard, Allen, Sterling (Henderson), Shelvey, Suarez, Borini (Suso).

United: Lindegaard, Rafael (Welbeck), Evra, Ferdinand, Evans, Valencia, Giggs, Carrick, Nani (Scholes), Kagawa (Chicharito), Van Persie.

Attendance: 44,263

13 January 2013

Manchester United 2 Liverpool 1

Although we didn't know it at the time, this would turn out to be the last United-Liverpool game Fergie oversaw as manager. Many will say of that final season that United won the league largely because of the failure of anyone else to mount a decent challenge. That ignores the total of 89 points the Reds managed to pile up, matching the total that city amassed to win the league a year earlier and one that had only been bettered five times since the Premier League began.

It's true to say that this wasn't a vintage United side. Van Persie was far and away the league's best player, aided in midfield by the league's best midfielder Michael Carrick, although few outside United's support (and some inside it) recognised this. However, there was no question that the star of this United effort was the manager, as indeed had pretty much been the case in all trophies won since the departure of Ronaldo. Fergie's experience, tactical nous and sheer will to win had been the crucial factor in securing the title wins since then and this final league title stands as a fitting tribute to his greatness. What other manager could deploy a midfielder like Tom Cleverley (incidentally, here he became the last player to make his bow in a United-Liverpool game under Ferguson) so effectively as to mask once again the side's shortage of quality in the centre of the park? United rarely dominated games for ninety minutes during this campaign, yet we possessed a winning mentality and an ability to make the very best of what we had to ensure we fell to only five defeats. We'd go on to be champions by a margin of eleven points.

The Reds went into this game on a nine game unbeaten run, though that had included heart-stopping encounters with Reading and Newcastle where we lost control of the game for long periods but ran out winners by the odd goal in seven. Even more crucial had been the 3-2 win at city, thanks to a Van Persie free kick in stoppage time. Roberto Mancini, increasingly struggling to get his side to perform at the level of the previous year, would go on to complain that, had they managed to sign the Dutchman, they'd have been top of the league by now. He was probably right, but such a remark could hardly have had a positive effect in the dressing room. It was another of those examples of a motivational error you couldn't ever imagine Fergie making.

Rodgers was rebuilding Liverpool and they would go on, surprisingly, to challenge for the league the following season, providing a rare moment of satisfaction for United fans in that awful first post-Fergie year when they blew it after the kind of premature celebrations the Liverpool of old would never have indulged in. There were certainly few signs of that thankfully brief renaissance here: defeat at Old Trafford would mean four losses in their last eight games, including a dismal home defeat to Aston Villa, and there would be many more inept performances as they limped to seventh place in the league. They'd already been knocked out of the League Cup at home to Swansea and were soon to fall to a hilarious defeat at Oldham in the FA Cup before Zenit St Petersburg effectively ended their season in February when they put them out of the Europa League in the first round of the knockout stage.

Here, they were outclassed by a United side who were now getting into the groove for what turned out to be a final assault on the title under Alex Ferguson. Van Persie gave us the lead when he steered an Evra cross into the net in the nineteenth minute: it was his ninth goal in ten Premier League games. In the second half he turned provider, his free kick finding Evra's head at the far post, though the ball deflected off Vidic on its way into the net.

United had been in control of the game throughout, although we gave Liverpool a lifeline when careless play in midfield allowed Gerrard to sneak in and get a shot on goal: it was parried by De Gea but Sturridge was there to fire home from the rebound and the same player might well have grabbed a point for the visitors had he not spurned an excellent opportunity to equalise late in the game.

United: De Gea, Rafael, Evra, Ferdinand, Vidic (Smalling), Carrick, Young (Valencia), Cleverley, Kagawa (Jones), Welbeck, Van Persie.

Liverpool: Reina, Johnson, Agger, Skrtel, Wisdom, Gerrard, Downing, Lucas (Sturridge), Allen (Henderson), Sterling (Borini), Suarez.

Attendance: 75,501

Performance Record (Ferguson v Rodgers)

Games – 2
United wins – 2
Draws – 0
Liverpool wins – 0
United goals – 4
Liverpool goals - 2

Honours

Manchester United – 1 Premier League
Liverpool – Fuck all

Transfer expenditure

Incoming transfers
Manchester United – £51 million
Liverpool – £49.5 million

Outgoing transfers
Manchester United – £4 million
Liverpool – £13 million

Net spend
Manchester United – £47 million
Liverpool – £36.5 million

References

1. A very good overview of the Peterloo massacre and its aftermath can be found at **https://en.wikipedia.org/wiki/Peterloo_Massacre**. For more in-depth coverage, see:
 R Reid, The Peterloo Massacre
J Marlowe, The Peterloo Massacre
M.Bush, The Casualties of Peterloo
2. **www.bbc.co.uk/sport/0/football/19694438**

Epilogue

May 2013

Three Days That Said: This Is How It Feels to be a Red

BELOW IS THE FULL TEXT AN ARTICLE I WROTE FOR THE RED MANCUNIAN WEBSITE IN MAY 2013. I'M RE-PRINTING IT IN ITS ORIGINAL VERSION HERE PARTLY BECAUSE IT SEEMS AN APPROPRIATE COMMENT ON THE END OF FERGIE'S REIGN AND PARTLY BECAUSE OF THE ONLINE ABUSE IT GENERATED FROM A NUMBER OF LIVERPOOL FANS. IT SEEMED, FRANKLY, TO TOUCH A NERVE.

The gulf between United and our main rivals has never been better illustrated than over the last few days. First, we had the enjoyable experience of watching city's mercenaries - twelve of whom cost more individually than Wigan's entire team - capitulate pitifully in the FA Cup Final, before the next day watching a United squad that included, amazingly, ten players who've been at the club since their teens, collecting their Premiership medals in one of the most vibrant Old Trafford atmospheres of recent times.

In a perfectly apposite sub-plot, we were of course also saying goodbye to a manager who's fulfilled footballing dreams we didn't even dare admit to ourselves prior to his arrival nearly 27 years ago. Even as Sir Alex was willing us to give the same support to our new manager that he had enjoyed, city were formulating their plans for replacing a manager who'd taken them to their first trophies in over three decades and who now was being sacked for 'failing to meet targets'.

The business terms they spoke in were perfectly apt. While we bemoan the corporate aspects of Manchester United that have intruded on the identity of our great club, both Sunday and that incredible parade on Monday showed that United are far more than that and always will be. The nouveau riche of city, however, are a club without soul, understanding concepts only like returns on investment, in-year projections and globalizing their brand, even though they don't really have one. Their fans chant the names of their financial godfathers in a way that any other club's fans would consider embarrassing, crass and entirely removed from the true spirit of the game.

Then there was that parade itself. Painting the town a glowing shade of Manchester Red were around seven times the number of supporters than had turned out to watch city parade their first championship trophy for 44 years last May. Some outsiders were taken aback by the spectacle, having happily bought into the myth that United don't enjoy a large home-town support. This view has never accorded with the facts and that so many were determined to find a way of taking part to say goodbye to Fergie provided a massive contrast to the furtive, back door exit of city's only successful manager in modern times.

Last night I was back at Old Trafford to watch our Under-21s take apart Liverpool in the semi-final of the Elite League competition. It wasn't just that we won 3-0 on the night: the way United's youngsters played the ball around was as much of a testimony to the wonderful club Fergie has built as were those title celebrations. Liverpool, in contrast, not only seemed to have given up on nurturing good footballing principles among their young players, but carried with them an all too familiar sense of irate indignation that has become the unmistakeable stamp of the Anfield club in recent years.

It's something I've written about in detail in my book *A Deeper Shade of Red*, which has, as expected, received some hostile reactions from Liverpool fans in its depiction of the club's growing persecution complex and victim fetish. Yet it was all too evident last night, where their players abandoned any attempt at playing football and constantly relied on the kind of tackles that would give Tony Pulis wet dreams, throwing up their arms in aggrieved horror and marching with wagging finger towards the ref whenever he rightly penalised them for it.

Two of these challenges resulted in penalties for United, masterfully converted by Larnell Cole, who grabbed a deserved hat trick later on, and were the result of exquisite build up play featuring the excellent Adnan Januzaj and Tom Lawrence: clearly Liverpool didn't have the footballing means to counter such threats and so resorted to hapless bullying tactics and evidently well practised whingeing when they didn't get away with them.

I don't know how many of those young lads in United shirts last night will make it at the top level (although I'd bet my house on Januzaj doing so, and I note that Michael Keane is now featuring in the first team squad page of the official website) but their schooling in playing the game the right way, in refusing to be intimidated in such circumstances and in their obvious pride in wearing that red shirt were overwhelmingly in evidence, and again stood in contrast to the modern version of the club who Fergie so magnificently knocked off their perch all those years ago.

Evidently, having been knocked off that perch, they're still rolling around the floor of the birdcage eking out an existence among the shit. And city, despite that fleeting dalliance with success last year, will always be down there with them.

Published: 5/5/13 at **http://redmancunian.com**

United v Liverpool in the Alex Ferguson Era

Overall record (United)

Played – 62
Wins – 30
Draws – 13
Defeats – 19
Goals For – 80
Goals Against - 69

Honours

United

2 UEFA Champions Leagues
13 Premier Leagues
5 FA Cups
4 League Cups
10 Charity/Community Shields (including one shared)
1 European Cup Winners' Cup
1 FIFA Club World Cup
1 European Super Cup
1 Intercontinental Cup

Liverpool

1 UEFA Champions League
2 League Championships
4 FA Cups
4 League Cups
5 FA Charity/Community Shields (including one shared)
1 UEFA Cup
2 European Super Cups

Most Appearances in United-Liverpool Games

United

44 – Ryan Giggs
33 – Paul Scholes
26 – Gary Neville
22 – Dennis Irwin
20 – Roy Keane
19 – David Beckham
19 – Steve Bruce
19 – Rio Ferdinand
19 – Gary Pallister
18 – Brian McClair

Liverpool

33 – Jamie Carragher
30 – Steven Gerrard
21 – Sami Hyypia
19 – Pepe Reina
18 – Ian Rush
17 – John Barnes
16 – Jamie Redknapp
16 – John-Arne Riise
16 – Steve McManaman
14 – Michael Owen

Most Goals in United-Liverpool Games

United

5 – Ryan Giggs
5 – Mark Hughes
4 – Andy Cole
4 – Wayne Rooney

Liverpool

7 – Steven Gerrard
6 – John Barnes
6 – Robbie Fowler
6 – Michael Owen
4 – Peter Beardsley
4 – Dirk Kuyt
4 – Danny Murphy

Most Red Cards in United-Liverpool Games

United
3 – Nemanja Vidic

Liverpool
2 – Javier Maschereno

Most Yellow Cards in United-Liverpool Games

United
9 – Roy Keane
8 – Paul Scholes
5 – Nemanja Vidic

Liverpool
12 – Jamie Carragher
6 – Jamie Redknapp
5 – Steven Gerrard
5 – Javier Mascherano

Home-grown players who featured in United-Liverpool games during the Ferguson era*

United – 33

Gary Walsh, Norman Whiteside, Mike Duxbury, Arthur Albiston, Clayton Blackmore, Billy Garton, Lee Martin, Russell Beardsmore, Mark Robins, Lee Sharpe, Mark Hughes, Ryan Giggs, Darren Ferguson, Nicky Butt, Gary Neville, Phil Neville, Paul Scholes, David Beckham, Ben Thornley, Michael Clegg, Ronnie Wallwork, Wes Brown, Luke Chadwick, John O'Shea, Michael Stewart, Darren Fletcher, Keiron Richardson, Jonny Evans, Federico Macheda, Darren Gibson, Rafael, Danny Welbeck, Tom Cleverley.

Liverpool – 16

Gary Ablett, Mike Marsh, Steve McManaman, Robbie Fowler, Dominic Matteo, Jamie Carragher, Michael Owen, David Thompson, Steven Gerrard, Stephen Wright, Stephen Warnock, Gary Kelly, Jay Spearing, Raheem Sterling, Suso, Andre Wisdom

*Players who were at the club at eighteen years old or younger. Inevitably there are some in this list, such as Lee Sharpe of United and Rahim Sterling of Liverpool, who joined from other clubs at or before that age.

Biggest transfer fees (paid) in Ferguson era*

(Millions)

United

£30.75 - Dimitar Berbatov
£28.1 – Juan Sebastian Veron
£27.55 – Rio Ferdinand
£25.9 – Wayne Rooney
£22.5 – Robin Van Persie
£19 – Ruud Van Nistelrooy

£18.9 – David De Gea
£18.6 – Michael Carrick
£17 - Anderson
£17 – Owen Hargreaves

Liverpool

£35 – Andy Carroll
£22.8 – Luis Suarez
£20.2 – Fernando Torres
£19 – Robbie Keane
£18.6 – Javier Mascherano
£18.5 – Stewart Downing
£17.5 – Glen Johnson
£17.1 – Alberto Aquilani
£16 – Jordan Henderson
£14.5 – Djibril Cisse

*For sources, see note on transfer information at the start of the book.

League positions by season in the Ferguson era

Season	United	Liverpool
1986-87	11	2
1987-88	2	1
1988-89	11	2
1989-90	13	1
1990-91	6	2
1991-92	2	6
1992-93	1	6
1993-94	1	8
1994-95	2	4
1995-96	1	3
1996-97	1	4
1997-98	2	3
1998-99	1	7
1999-2000	1	4
2000-01	1	3
2001-02	3	2
2002-03	1	5
2003-04	3	4
2004-05	3	5
2005-06	2	3
2006-07	1	3
2007-08	1	4
2008-09	1	2
2009-10	2	7
2010-11	1	6
2011-12	2	8
2012-13	1	7

Average attendances by season in the

Ferguson era

Source: **www.european-football-statistics.co.uk/attn.htm**

Season	United	Liverpool
1986-87	50,594	36,286
1987-88	39,152	39,582
1988-89	36,488	38,574
1989-90	39.077	36,589
1990-91	43,218	36,864
1991-92	44,984	34,799
1992-93	35,152	37,004
1993-94	44,244	38,493
1994-95	43,681	34,176
1995-96	41,700	39,553
1996-97	55,081	39,777
1997-98	55,168	40,628
1998-99	55,188	43,321
1999-2000	58,014	44,074
2000-01	67,490	43,699
2001-02	67,558	43,389
2002-03	67,602	43,243
2003-04	67,641	42,706
2004-05	67,748	42,587
2005-06	68,765	44,236
2006-07	75,826	43,561
2007-08	75,691	43,532
2008-09	75,304	43,611
2009-10	74,864	42,864
2010-11	75, 109	42,820
2011-12	75,387	44,253
2012-13	75,530	44,749

Selected Bibliography

Phillip Auclair, Cantona – The Rebel Who Would Be King
Patrick Barclay, Football: Bloody Hell
Michael Crick & David Smith, Manchester United – The Betrayal of a Legend
Sean Egan, The Doc's Devils – Manchester United 1972-1977
Alex Ferguson,Leading
Alex Ferguson, My Autobiography
Dave Hill, Out of His Skin
Tim Howard, The Keeper: A Life of Saving Goals and Achieving Them
Leo Moynihan, Gordon Strachan
Gary Neville, Red
Robert Reid, The Peterloo Massacre
Norman Whiteside, Whiteside

Made in the USA
Lexington, KY
10 December 2017